DATE DUE

Reading real books

RETHINKING READING

Series Editor: L. John Chapman
School of Education, The Open University

Reading real books

ROBIN CAMPBELL

Open University Press
Buckingham · Philadelphia

Open University Press
Celtic Court
22 Ballmoor
Buckingham
MK18 1XW

and
1900 Frost Road, Suite 101
Bristol, PA 19007, USA

First Published 1992

A catalogue record of this book is available
from the British Library

Library of Congress Cataloging-in-Publication Data

Campbell, Robin, 1937–
    Reading real books / Robin Campbell.
        p.   cm. — (Rethinking reading)
    Includes bibliographical references and index.
    ISBN 0-335-15794-7   ISBN 0-335-15793-9 (pbk)
    1. Reading (Elementary)—Language experience approach.
2. Children—Books and reading.   I. Title.   II. Series.
LB1573.33.C36   1992
372.4—dc20   92-8263
                                                                                        CIP

1683159   *2-7-94*

Typeset by Inforum, Rowlands Castle, Hants
Printed in Great Britain by St Edmundsbury Press,
Bury St Edmunds, Suffolk

Contents

Acknowledgements

Throughout the writing of this book politicians and journalists have been having a field day commenting upon the adequacy, or otherwise, of various approaches to the teaching of reading. In the meantime, parents, teachers, student teachers and teacher educators have been continuing with their efforts to encourage the reading development of young children. This book has been written as a support for those efforts and as an attempt to illuminate the debate about a particular approach which is known as 'real books'.

The evidence for this support is drawn from various sources. First, there are the numerous classes that have been visited where teachers and children have been seen working effectively with the approach. Then, there is the writing of Ken and Yetta Goodman, Margaret Meek, Brian Cambourne, Don Holdaway, etc., which adds weight to the argument. Third, there are the comments and questions raised by professional colleagues which serve to clarify some of the issues. Making sense of all of that is facilitated by the support that I receive from my wife, Ruby, and the rest of my family.

Part of this book involves the use of text from story books. The author and publisher would like to thank the following for permission to reproduce copyright material in this book: The Bodley Head, *Rosie's Walk* by Pat Hutchins; and Philomel Books and Hamish Hamilton's Children's Books, *The Very Hungry Caterpillar* by Eric Carle.

CHAPTER 1

Introduction

Teachers of young children consider the teaching of reading to be of great importance. As part of encouraging children's reading development the questions of which books to use in the classroom and how to teach the children to read assume considerable importance for teachers. Indeed *The Great Debate*, as Chall (1967) refers to it, has raged for decades, if not centuries, and looks like continuing for some time to come. The debate on those two central concerns of books and methods is often heated, both in schools and in the educational press. More recently, the debate has spilled over to the public arena, as it does from time to time, and has centred on the issue of real books.

Now at first sight the term 'real books', would appear to suggest a debate about the books to be made available to young beginning readers. However, as we shall see, the term is indicative not only of the books to be read but also of the methods to be used and of the teaching and learning environment to be provided. There is, then, a philosophy of teaching and learning which underpins the term 'real books' and extends those words far beyond the selection of texts to be provided in the classroom. In the USA, Goodman (1986) utilizes the term 'whole language' to encompass a relatively similar philosophy of teaching and learning.

And 'whole language', 'story books', 'literature-based learning' or 'meaningful books' might have been better terms to use. However, 'real books' is the way in which this particular approach to reading has been described by many teachers and educators and is the term at the centre of the argument in the UK. It is therefore used in this text. And, of course, although the term is important, what is more important is to consider what the term actually means for children as developing readers and for teachers in the classroom.

But why the public interest in real books during the early years of the 1990s? It probably stems, in the UK, from the publication of *Sponsored*

Reading Failure (Turner, 1990) and the immediate dissemination of that work by the national press, radio and television. Martin Turner, an educational psychologist, published the reading test results of primary school children from nine local education authorities. Those results, he argued, demonstrated that there had been a downturn in the reading attainment of young children during the second half of the 1980s. And he postulated that the downturn could be linked to the real books movement which teachers of infants had embraced in that period.

Informed opinion questioned a number of the claims made by Turner. The presentation of the statistical data was regarded as inadequate (Cashdan, 1990); indeed, the tests which were used were regarded as questionable (Dombey, 1990). Furthermore, it was felt that the limited extent to which young children were familiar with taking tests could influence the results (Harrison, 1991). And the link which was made between the results and real books was regarded as 'absurd' (Cox, 1990). Certainly there appeared to be no clear evidence on the teaching methods used in the schools that were purported to be witnessing a downturn in reading standards (Campbell, 1990b). Yet none of these views were capable of limiting the continuing attacks, on teachers in general and on real books in particular, in the national arena.

So did the real books approach deserve such a bad press? Probably not. If there had been any downturn in reading standards then real books could hardly be blamed, as Her Majesty's Inspectors of Schools in a subsequent survey found only 5 per cent of teachers who described their approach as exclusively that of real books (HMI, 1990). Furthermore, there was some indication that those teachers were expressing a very limited, even false, view of what constitutes a real books appproach. That is, they were emphasizing the provision of the real books and the repeated sharings of those books as the means by which the children would be encouraged to read. Now, of course, the provision of real books and shared readings is an important feature of a real books approach. However, it is far too simplistic to suggest that is all there is to this approach. It is also incorrect to suggest that the approach is one of minimalist teaching, although some articles in the national press labelled it as a 'non-teaching movement' (Phillips, 1990). Indeed many teachers would regard a real books approach as a very demanding one which requires subtle and sophisticated teaching strategies and a prior careful planning of the classroom environment to facilitate the management of learning. So, what are the main features of a real books approach to early reading development?

The approach does have as a basis real books and shared readings. Therefore there are immediately four crucial elements: the books; the child; the teacher; and the interaction centred on a book, which brings together the learner and the teacher.

The books that provide the basis for the child's readings have been refered to as 'real books', as a contrast to those books which many children refer to as 'reading books' and which teachers and parents know as 'scheme books' or 'basals'. The important feature of such real books or stories is that they are meaningful to the child. And they are meaningful because there is a real story to tell, the language is natural rather than controlled, and the reading is aided because predictions can be made by the reader and/or listener (Wade, 1990). Of course, when such criteria are applied to books it becomes apparent that not all books within all schemes would fail the test (Donaldson, 1989). Nevertheless, what remains is the notion of the power of stories to encourage and facilitate children's reading development.

However, it is not only the power of stories that facilitates the reading development of the young child. Children bring to the task of reading a variety of language and experiences, and a curiosity to find out about the world around them. They are self-activated to learn (Wells, 1985) and have been attempting to make sense of their environment and the objects in that environment from a very early age. Part of that making sense of the environment will be to come to terms with the print which is all around them. Children will, therefore, have learnt a great deal about reading before they are reading in the conventional sense of that word (Ferreiro and Teberosky, 1982). All of that knowledge about language, print and the environment will provide a basis for the child's explorations of books. And if the books are predictable natural texts then the child's active involvement with, and reconstruction of, the book will be aided.

Of course, the children will be assisted in their explorations of books if a teacher works alongside them. So shared readings become an important part of the real books approach. Both Meek (1982) and Smith (1978) have argued the importance of the book, the child and the teacher as the factors needed to encourage reading development. And it is here that the teacher's role becomes important. The teacher is part of the process not as passive listener but rather as active participant. In early shared readings the teacher might read the story to the child and encourage the child to retell the story, support the child in his/her attempt to read on his/her own or enable the child to read alongside the teacher. In such an apprenticeship approach (Waterland, 1988) the role of the teacher and of the child will be constantly evolving. Subsequently, the teacher will listen to the child read, compare that reading to the text, making judgements as to the amount of support the child requires, and then provide that support or teaching which helps the child immediately and perhaps suggests strategies for the future. It is difficult, therefore, to see a real books approach as one which might be regarded as a non-teaching approach to reading. A belief in the power of stories and of children as active constructors of learning does not necessarily imply a belief in non-teaching.

Furthermore, the bringing together of a book, a child and a teacher into a worthwhile interaction will take other forms besides that of shared readings (Campbell,1990a). Story readings, hearing a child read and some form of sustained silent reading are all literacy events which will support learners in their development as readers. And each of those interactions will require varying teacher strategies to meet the differing needs of the children. Such a view reinforces a real books approach as one which, rather than indicating non-teaching, actually emphasizes the importance of the teacher.

That importance of the teacher is evident during literacy-event inter-actions. However, it is evident also in the prior organization of the class-room without which the literacy events could not take place or would be less effective when they did occur. Therefore, the teacher adopting a real books approach will organize the classroom so that the children can engage in worthwhile activities, occasionally independently, and the teacher will be able to be involved in one-to-one literacy-event interactions. Among the various arrangements that the teacher will provide will be a number that contribute to literacy development. So a writing centre, a listening area and a library corner will all be evident. There will also be a good deal of print on display around the room; the environment of the classroom will replicate the external environment in emphasizing the im-portance of print. The National Curriculum in the UK encourages such a print-rich classroom for young children (DES, 1990). However the prior organization of the classroom would in itself be insufficient without the careful management of the class throughout the school day. The teacher plans and organizes so that subsequently children can be guided, sup-ported, and encouraged.

The teacher, and the school policy, will also recognize the importance of home–school links. Indeed, Davis and Stubbs (1988) emphasized the role of parental involvement in shared reading interactions. In part, that suggestion was based on the quality of the interaction that might be pro-vided by the parent with just one child to consider. But it was also an appropriate recognition of the role of the parent as a major contributor to the child's literacy development both before the child starts schooling and once enrolled at school. Nevertheless, the links between home and school have to be nurtured carefully and teachers have an important task to ensure that the communications between school and home are appropri-ate to encourage a genuine collaboration.

Although the majority of teachers of young children would emphasize the importance of literacy development, nevertheless that literacy develop-ment does not take place in a vacuum. So not only will stories provide a rich source of beginnings for reading and writing; the interests of the children, together with the school and the wider environment, will also provide the starting point for literacy activities. A language experience approach (God-dard,1974) and thematic work serve to meet the interests of the children. Scientific experiments, caring for pets, visits, drama, play, painting and model-making all provide a stimulus for reading activities. And those activities also create the opportunities for writing, in a variety of registers, both for self and others.

The making of connections between reading and writing is an important feature of the real books approach. Reading and writing support each other. The child who is receiving encouragement to read will want to explore the act of writing. The child who begins to produce some writing will begin to understand more about the print that is contained within books. And the teacher can encourage the making of those connections by supporting children's efforts to write for others so that an understanding of purpose and audience is established.

Throughout all of the above literacy activities the teacher will have been engaged in interactions with the children or will have been observing the children during the process of writing. Those interactions and observations allow teachers to acquire a fund of information about children's literacy development. As is argued for whole language teachers in the USA (Goodman *et al.*, 1989) so, too, teachers following the similar real books approach in the UK can use that fund of information to analyse and evaluate each child's literacy development.

What will have become very evident is that, although this book is about real books in the infant classroom, it does not adopt a narrow interpretation of the term 'real books'. Indeed, the view that is put forward in this text is that teachers working within a real books approach use those books as a starting point for a whole range of literacy activities. And they do so because using real books implies an approach to teaching and learning which encapsulates far more than the choice of books in the classroom. Therefore any teacher, or school, that begins to use real books has to change far more than the books that are provided for the children (Coles, 1990). So home–school links, classroom organization, the use of environmental print, various classroom interactions, writing, thematic work and assessment are all areas that require careful consideration.

Nevertheless real books, as a source for reading, are an important starting place. Therefore, Chapter 2 will consider real books. It will do so in the context of an exploration of reading schemes, the notion of the power of stories and of the language and experience that children bring to the task.

Later chapters will deal with aspects of the real books approach. Linking to real books, as the material to be read, Chapter 3 will explore shared reading in the classroom and consider the varieties of that interaction as each child develops as a reader.

Home–school links provide the basis of Chapter 4. In particular, attention will be given to the efforts that have been made by some schools to establish collaborative support for the efforts of the child.

Back in the school there is the need to consider, in Chapter 5, the organization and management that teachers provide in the classroom, within the framework of a school policy, in order to facilitate literacy growth. Part of that organization entails the use of environmental and classroom print (Chapter 6).

The discussion will then return to the use of real books but in other literacy events. Chapter 7 will consider the importance of story readings and Chapter 8 other classroom interactions centred upon a book, such as shared readings in a group with a big book, hearing a child read, sustained silent reading and the use of nursery rhymes and songs.

The books can also be the starting point for making reading and writing connections. Those connections and other writing opportunities are considered in Chapter 9. Of course, some of that writing and reading will be derived from thematic work and/or language experience approaches; those aspects will be discussed in Chapter 10.

Assessment now forms an important feature of primary school work and is formalized within the teacher assessments and the standardized assessment tasks of the National Curriculum in the UK (DES, 1990). But teachers are observing, interacting, recording, analysing and evaluating throughout the school year. Indeed, all of that is the basis for subsequent planning. It will be debated in Chapter 11.

Finally, in Chapter 12, the important roles of the teacher will be brought together. That chapter will serve to emphasize that a real books approach is not a non-teaching approach. Although the importance of the teacher should be self-evident by that stage, nevertheless it will be worth underlining the point.

CHAPTER 2

Real books

It has been suggested already that real books, as an approach to early literacy development, should be seen as something which takes us well beyond the materials to be read; nevertheless, the books to be read are central to the approach in primary classrooms. And those books are regarded as being real books because they will be those written with a story to tell and using natural language. That is in contrast to those books written with the express purpose of teaching children to read and which might, therefore, use a controlled vocabulary, with a systematic repetition of that vocabulary, and simplified sentences. Which is not to say that all reading-scheme books, or basals, should be discounted (Donaldson, 1989), but they should be examined for their literary merits.

The real books approach was, then, in part a response to the inade quacies of the language and content of reading schemes. However, the emphasis upon real books was not just that. Real books also recognized the power of stories, or of the centrality of narrative in the early years of literacy development (Whitehead, 1988). That emphasis upon story is stressed by writers such as Meek (1982; 1988) and Wade (1990), both of whom are regarded, by exponents and critics of real books, as being at the forefront of the real books approach in the UK. Furthermore, the stress upon the use of real books was also related to an increasing awareness of the extent to which children bring to the task of learning to read a variety of language, experiences and expectations which might be most readily matched by natural language texts. In particular, the work of Goodman (see, for instance, his collection of writing in Gollasch, 1982) and Smith (e.g., 1978), in North America, have been influential in this development.

Each of those aspects, namely, reading schemes, real books and the power of stories, and children as literacy learners, requires greater consideration. And the starting point for our explorations might usefully be reading schemes.

Reading schemes

Perhaps the first point that should be made is that reading schemes in a variety of formats and with an emphasis upon a phonics approach or a whole-word or look-and-say-methodology have been used for many years and many children have learnt to read with those schemes. It is a point that is conceded by Smith (1978, p.4):

> In the two-thousand year recorded history of reading instruction, as far as I have been able to discover, no-one has devised a method of teaching reading that has not proved a success with some children.

Children have learnt to read with reading schemes, although whether that is because of, or despite, the method employed is more contentious. The issue is that teachers are providing a whole range of literacy experiences, materials and teaching. The exact reason for children's successes or failures, therefore, is often difficult to determine. However, even though reading schemes have been used with some success, the question that has to be raised is whether these books are the best that might be used.

It is, of course, relatively easy to be critical of some reading schemes. In particular, attempts to make reading easy for the learner has in the past produced such pages as the following by M'Culloch (1852, p.11):

> In it.
> Up at it.
> Up at us.
> On us.
> An ox.
> On an ox.
> I am on an ox.
> Up on it.
> On, up-on an ox.

Such pages would appear to be more of a tongue twister than a support for a young child learning to read. However, it is possible to see how the author was attempting to help the child. Key features of a reading scheme such as a controlled vocabulary, to lessen the demand on the child, repetition of the vocabulary, as a reinforcement of the learning process, and simplified short sentences, to match the child's relatively short sentences, are all apparent. In addition, in this text there is the attempted simplification by limiting the vocabulary to words of just two letters. Nevertheless, the outcome is surely that the child is left to produce a reading almost solely dependent upon a knowledge of letters and sounds and/or of word recognition. The important support that sentence structure and meaning can provide for a young reader is very largely not available in such texts, at least in the earliest pages.

The development within such a scheme was to move subsequently to pages of text with nothing in excess of three letter words and, if phonic based, to emphasize such aspects as short vowels preceded and followed by a consonant, as in the following text from M'Culloch (1852, p.13):

> It is my bag.
> He is a wag.
> Is the pad on the nag?
> A fat rat.
> A fat ham in the bag.
> Sam has a hat on.
> He is a bad lad.
> Dan has to pat the ram.
> She sat on the mat; as the rat ran.
> My hat is in the bag on my lap.
> She has the fan in my bag.
> I am to go in the van.
> She had a fan.
> I had a bag.

So as the text is extended the child was given some syntactic support and some semantic support within each sentence. There was, however, very little if any connection between the sentences. It is difficult, for the reader, to predict the development of the discourse.

Of course, the examples that have been given of a reading scheme were taken from the last century and undoubtedly it could be claimed that there have been substantial advances in reading schemes since that time. Nevertheless, in his critique of reading schemes Wade (1990) utilized a more recent example to demonstrate some of the problems which continue to be associated with such texts. The simple vocabulary, the repetition of words but also of sounds and ideas, and short sentences all remain features of scheme books. But, more importantly, Wade questioned the cohesion and coherence of reading-scheme texts. Making connections between the events and episodes may often be as difficult as in the example above of Dan and Sam.

In order to emphasize that lack of connection Wade used a particularly interesting strategy. He presented eighteen lines of reading-scheme text and then debated those lines in some detail. And only when the reader was made aware of some of the problems of the text did he reveal that the eighteen lines had been presented in exactly the reverse order from the original book. Children may be denied the important support that can come from forward-moving narrative, where meaning is developed, when texts can be reversed with so little effect upon the sense of the prose.

It is not difficult, in such circumstances, to see why an emphasis upon reading materials which contained natural language became prominent. Clay (1972) reported upon the use of natural language texts in New Zealand and contrasted them with earlier stilted texts. These new texts were developed without the controlling imperatives of vocabulary and sentences, at least as previously used. Now the important feature had become that of retaining the qualities and cues of children's natural language. Although graded and in a scheme, the books nevertheless emphasized the language with which the children were familiar and where meaning throughout each of the books was considered to be important.

Nevertheless, although some might be concerned with the notion of books within a scheme, the crucial issue in determining the value of a book must be whether it is meaningful as a text to the young reader. Donaldson (1989) argued that scheme books should not be rejected solely on the basis that they are in a scheme. Instead, she suggested we might use the criteria offered by Meek (1982) that the pictures help the reader to understand the story, that the story has a shape and that the author has a voice. Those criteria will help create a book which will be meaningful for many readers.

The role of the pictures in helping the reader understand the story is an area that is explored in some depth by Graham (1991). She argued that reading schemes in particular often would stick to the text so tightly and so literally that it would leave no room for interpretation. As a contrast she draws upon the example of *Rosie's Walk* (Hutchins, 1969) to remind us of the way in which what is left unsaid in the story is so clearly described in the pictures. (*Rosie's Walk* is surely one of the most loved of infant classroom stories and one of the books most frequently written about in texts on early reading: see, for example, Meek, 1988; Money, 1988; Wade, 1990; and later in this book). Graham also draws upon numerous other examples to demonstrate how illustrations can help the reader understand the story in real books.

In many instances the first story books read to, or by, children will be rich in rhyme, rhythm and repetition (Wade,1990). An exploration of the many nursery rhymes that children might encounter will demonstrate those elements and remind us of how they capture the child's attention and imagination. And, of course, the repetition is used here to emphasize meaning and give shape, rather than to control vocabulary as it might in a reading scheme.

Nevertheless, because there are these criteria by which real books might be judged, there is also a need to be careful with books that are not part of reading schemes. Just as not all reading scheme books need necessarily be rejected so, too, not all books outside schemes need necessarily be accepted. Pearson (1990) provided an exploration of two books, one from a reading scheme and the other a possible real book. Even though, for example, both of the books contained repetition, Pearson concluded that the particular reading-scheme book which he examined was a rich and humorous story and that the non-scheme book was a dull and uneventful text.

What becomes apparent, then, is that although many reading scheme books might be rejected as being unsuitable as early reading material for young children, some non-scheme books might also be rejected as being unsuitable. The role of the teacher is to make a careful selection of well-illustrated books with good storylines written by an author in a natural language so that the book will be of interest and meaningful to the child. These real books then provide the basis for a number of literacy activities and for the child's continuing literacy development. However, before considering some of those activities we need to consider two other features. The first of these concerns the use of real books and the centrality of narrative, or the power of stories, in literacy development during the early years of education.

Real books and the power of stories

The importance of the books to be read and the power of stories in children's lives can perhaps be best viewed from two perspectives. First, there is the role of story or narrative as part of a childhood culture with an oral tradition. Second, there is the importance of story which encourages development in language, thinking and feelings.

Wade (1990), in particular, draws upon the work of Iona and Peter Opie (1959) in order to demonstrate how the culture of childhood is embedded in an oral tradition. A range of activites and games structured by language, and frequently in a narrative form, are passed from one generation of children to another. For instance, in one skipping game there is the narrative:

> Katie in the kitchen
> Doing a bit of stitching
> In comes the Bogie Man
> And out goes Katie.

The story/rhyme structures and guides the activity. It also determines in this example the turn taking for skipping: a first named child (Katie) skips, then 'In comes' a second child to skip, and 'out goes' the first skipper. That narrative, and others like it for skipping, clapping and jumping games, structures the play but also enables children to develop their use of language and their knowledge of story structure. It means, in addition, that when the children move from these games to books they have an expectation and understanding of story to help them in their literacy development.

Already, for instance, they will have been learning that stories do not always work at the literal level. And that as well as giving shape and order to their experiences, stories can be associated with pleasure.

It is important, therefore, that the stories the children meet in the books, that are read to them by parents and teachers and subsequently that are read by the children themselves, continue to provide a stimulus to their language, thinking and feelings.

Meek (1988) demonstrated how children can learn from stories about the nature and variety of written discourse. Indeed, Meek argued that stories are a lesson of a kind. And in her close analysis of Ben reading *Rosie's Walk*, with a teacher acting as guide, she is able to indicate the reality of that statement. Of course, the child will be able to learn about sounds, words, rhythms and sentence structures through hearing and reading a variety of stories. But that learning about language will be extended to an awareness and knowledge about the structure of stories, the use of metaphor to create new meanings and, as a variety of genres are provided, the discourse styles of various genres.

Furthermore, in her example of Ben reading *Rosie's Walk*, Meek demonstrated how the young child can learn other lessons about reading a book. So gaining an understanding of authorship, audience, illustrations and iconic interpretation were all part of the child's literary growth. And classroom teachers will know of the importance of the child learning about authorship. Once a child becomes aware of author, and the possibility of other texts written by the same author, then a range of stories provide a substantial motivation for further reading.

If real books or stories were to achieve nothing more than these growths in language then they would already have achieved sufficient to win the argument. However, they do more, for the stories can also be important as a stimulus to thinking and feelings. Meek utilizes the work of Bruner (1986) to suggest that the author recruits the child's imagination by offering that which is familiar but doing so in a new guise, or by extending the real in some logical manner. Children as readers have, then, to provide an interpretation or explanation of the reading that takes them beyond the actual text. As Whitehead (1988) argued, stories provide a bridge to abstract thinking and to hypothesizing. They do so because stories are not always written at a purely literal level.

And yet there is more still, for the variety of stories can provide insights into a cultural heritage. Stories can initiate children not only into historical and geographical explorations but also into moral and religious issues. And they do so in ways which encourage the child to predict, consider and reflect upon the complexities of external events within the safety of a book. So the child's emotions are also touched by story. Indeed, one of the starting points for a real books approach is that feelings of pleasure are associated with listening to, joining in with and reading stories. In particular, that is true where nursery rhymes, with their rhythms, repetitions and predictabilities, are a part of the first source of stories in the classroom, because they provide a link to the oral tradition of the childhood culture.

The use of real books as a starting point is also important when consideration is given to what the learner brings to the task of reading and how texts can support the reader. So let us consider these features before moving into the literacy activities of the classroom.

Children as literacy learners

Although the real books approach in the primary classroom may be centred on various interactions or literacy events which recognize the importance of the teacher and the book, there is also an important recognition of what the child brings to the process. Those abilities, expectations and interests can be met by the use of appropriate books.

Children, in almost all cases, will have learnt to understand spoken language in some form or other by the time they reach school (Smith, 1978). That means they will know how language works, not in the sense of being able to articulate their knowledge by giving descriptions and explanations of language, but as demonstrated in their use of language. Furthermore, their experiences of the childhood culture of oral stories, and of oral interactions with adults sometimes centred on a story, will mean that the children have certain expectations of language and subsequently of literacy. Fox (1988) demonstrated the complexities and subtleties of the stories to which young children (3½–6 years of age) were able to relate. That ability enables children to understand the nature of real books and therefore to be able to predict and hypothesize through those stories.

Children are able to work in that intelligent manner because they come to the task of reading as active constructors of reality. Using a Piagetian perspective and based on studies of young children learning literacy, Ferreiro (1990) suggested that children can be seen to be intelligent, active and creative in both reading and writing. Such a view had been put forward earlier by Donaldson (1978), and although subsequently she questioned aspects of the real books approach (Donaldson, 1989), nevertheless her view remained that children are 'highly active and efficient learners, competent inquirers, eager to understand' (1989, p.5).

Children, then, can be regarded as self-activated learners (Wells, 1985) who attempt to make coherent the literacy systems. But that is no reason to leave them to find out for themselves. The books that are provided and the support that is given by the teacher are there to facilitate the learning.

Real books help the children read because they are written in a natural language, with predictable events and in a discourse pattern that the children have come to know. The complexities of learning to read are not made more complex by first of all having to learn a new set of rules which apply to the construction of reading scheme texts. Instead, the child can make almost immediate use of the semantic and syntactic cue systems, and increasingly use of the graphophonic cue system, in order to develop as a reader.

Goodman (1967) highlighted children's use of those three cue systems in his important paper on reading as a 'psycholinguistic guessing game' (but really 'hypothesis testing' or 'tentative information processing' rather than 'guessing' in the literal sense of that word). It is the semantic cues which provide the first connection for the young child. After all, the child will assume that the real book should provide a meaningful story. Therefore, the text and the illustrations should enable the child to match the book to his/her expectations and predictions and maintain the storyline.

So, in *The Naughty Sheep* (Amery and Cartwright, 1989), when Woolly the sheep

stops eating and looks over the . . . ,

both text and illustration support the reader to predict 'wire' or 'gate' or 'fence'. But it is not only the meaning or semantic cues that help. The child also has a considerable knowledge of syntax. The child's knowledge of sentence structure will assist in the reading of

Woolly stops eating and looks over the . . . .

The reader may not be able to talk about nouns but will be able to predict that the next word in the sentence might be that sort of word because that is how the child has come to understand that a sentence would be constructed.

Woolly stops eating and looks over the (a)

and

Woolly stops eating and looks over the (going)

are not acceptable alternatives for the reader. Therefore, the syntactic cues within the text will be helping the reader.

Finally, the child will also be using the graphophonic cueing system in order to help in the reading of the book. In particular, the child may make use of the first letter, and its associated sound, in order to hypothesize what the word might be (Campbell, 1987). So if the reader meets

Woolly stops eating and looks over the f . . .

then a recognition of the letter 'f', and a knowledge of the sound corresponding to that letter, will assist the reader in making an appropriate prediction.

Of course, the three cueing systems are not used in isolation from one another. The reader will be using all three cueing systems simultaneously. Therefore, with the support from semantic, syntactic and graphophonic cues, together with any information from illustrations in early reading books and with the knowledge and experiences that the reader brings to the task, there is a strong possibility that the reader will be able to predict that

Woolly stops eating and looks over the fence.

However, that appropriate reading is very much aided by being able to read a book which provides contextual support. So books which give powerful semantic and syntactic cues are to be preferred. They are real books rather than reading-scheme books (if that means stilted language, controlled vocabulary and oversimplified, unnatural sentences). These real books, storybooks or literature, provide a good match for the self-activated child learner.

Of course, the learner is not left to work alone with a real book. It is widely recognized that shared reading plays a very important part in the real books approach (see, for example Davis and Stubbs, 1988; Waterland, 1988; Campbell, 1990a). We therefore need to consider what is involved in shared reading, and will do so in the next chapter.

CHAPTER 3

Shared reading

Shared reading plays a very important part in the real books approach. In his argument against a skills approach to reading, Smith (1978) suggested that there were two basic preconditions for learning to read. First, there has to be an availability of materials which are interesting and make sense to the learner. Smith then proceeded to list a wide range of texts, from books, magazines, newspapers and comics to numerous examples of environmental print such as street signs, television commercials, labels, wrappers, notices, menus, timetables and so on. All of those materials have a part to play, but real books/stories/narratives may have a special role to play for the reasons already stated in Chapter 2. However, such materials may be insufficient on their own and the second precondition, therefore, is an understanding adult to act as a guide for the child's encounters with these various forms of print.

Meek (1982) expressed a similar view when she indicated that the key aspects for reading success were a book, the child and an adult (in the role of teacher) brought together in shared enjoyment of the story. Furthermore, an aspect of those shared readings is that the child is encouraged to produce, gradually, more of the reading as his/her development permits. On that basis shared reading has been defined as 'the interaction of an adult reading with a learner and encouraging and facilitating an increasingly more prominent reading role for the learner' (Campbell, 1990a, p.26).

Of course, definitions of shared reading, in UK primary schools, as a one-to-one interaction differs from other classroom suggestions for shared book experiences. Holdaway (1979) in New Zealand, for instance, provided details of shared readings with a big book where the interaction was of the teacher with a group. Such interactions are important and will be considered in Chapter 8. However, at this point we need to consider the key features, the sequence and the reality of the one-to-one shared reading interactions which have become such an important part of the real books approach.

It will already be apparent that the key features are contained within the book, the child, the teacher and the interaction. Some attention has already been given to two of those features: the book is a real book with natural language and of interest and meaningful to the child; the child is an active learner and will develop as a reader by reading. But that development requires guidance and it is here that the teacher has a key role.

The teacher may read the story to the learner during early shared readings. Therefore, an important feature of the shared readings is the model of reading that the teacher provides (Martin, 1989). However, the teacher does far more than just providing a model of reading. As Dombey (1987) argued, the teaching that is given during shared reading is complex and subtle. The teacher will read the story to the child, read alongside the child and support the child when he/she is reading. That support will require the teacher to tolerate restarts and meaningful miscues, wait for the child to self-correct, and provide mediations when the child requires more direct support. However, these mediations not only need to support the reader at that stage in the reading but also need to keep the child as an active learner and suggest appropriate strategies, whenever possible, for future readings. The teacher is therefore sustaining, encouraging and facilitating the learner in his/her self-activated learning (Wells, 1985).

The nature of the interaction will, in part, be determined by the role of the teacher. And Wells goes on to argue the importance of a genuine sharing and collaboration in such interactions. Waterland (1988) suggests that a simple, yet important, feature of shared reading is that it can be thought of as reading 'with me'. It is reading *together with* rather than more traditional reading *to* the teacher. Where the nature of the interaction is genuinely collaborative, then the likelihood is that it will provide a pleasurable experience for the child. However, an interaction that is enjoyable does not necessarily have to be intellectually undemanding (Whitehead, 1987). The child is being encouraged towards understanding the complexities of written language.

So what might a shared reading look like if a recording and transcription were made of a teacher and a child reading together? The answer to that question is that a variety of interactions might be expected. The exact nature of the interaction will, in particular, be determined by the child's progress and by the familiarity and complexity of the book that forms the basis for the interaction. Nevertheless, it is possible to indicate some sort of sequence which might be evident in that variety of shared readings.

First, there will be those occasions when the teacher reads the book to the child and the child makes no direct contribution to the reading. Of course, the child might make comments about the story or relate the story to his/her own life experiences. And some children might wish to retell the story in their own words after the teacher has completed the reading. Such comments and retellings will demonstrate the child's interest in the story and growing awareness of written language.

Second, the teacher might read the story to the child, with the child then rereading the story to the teacher. Such readings by the child are unlikely to be an exact reading of the print. The child might convey the general structure of the story, with a few variations, but pay limited attention to the precise wording. These emergent readings may be an important preliminary stage before a move towards more conventional readings (Teale, 1988). And that move from emergent readings to more conventional readings can be encouraged by the support that is given by the teacher during the shared readings.

Third, the reading of the book by the teacher to the child becomes more of a reading alongside each other. So at times the child will come into the reading and echo the teachers words. Aware of this, the teacher will occasionally fade out of the reading and therefore encourage the child to take over as leader. That will be the case especially where the flow of the language in the real book enables the child to predict the text with some ease. At times the teacher will follow the child's reading and echo his/her words; such a strategy appears to encourage and support the reader. It does provide confirmation to the reader that the predictions that are being made are appropriate. A particular feature of this reading alongside one another is the way in which there is a move from the teacher to the child leading the reading. And this comes about not because of any overt direction being given but because the teacher and the learner are in tune with each other's intentions. There is a true sharing and collaboration.

Fourth, as the child becomes more confident and independent as a reader he/she will begin to produce a more conventional reading of the book. The teacher will support such conventional readings by mediating from time to time as miscues are produced, although, of course, not all miscues will be mediated by the teacher. Judgements will be made by the teacher as to how the reader is progressing, the nature of the miscue, the extent to which meaning is being maintained and the time required by the reader to self-correct. On the basis of such analyses the teacher will support the child's reading with a variety of strategies.

Of course, the sequence is nowhere near as neat and tidy as might be suggested above. The teacher may or may not precede the child's retelling, emergent reading, reading alongside and conventional reading by reading the story to the child. In part, that might be determined by the number of times the child has heard the story. The familiarity of the child with the book will, therefore, influence the role of the teacher and will also mean that the child who usually provides an emergent reading might with a particular book provide a more conventional reading. Furthermore, the sequence is not so neat and tidy because the teacher and child are not restricted by the notion of four stages. A child might begin to provide an emergent reading then produce a page of conventional reading before reading alongside the teacher for a short period. The nature of the interaction and the roles of the child and the teacher will alter according to the needs which become evident within any one shared reading.

However, perhaps the most effective way of exploring the way in which teachers share books with children is to consider one complete shared reading interaction. The example is of five-year-old Richard sharing a book with his classteacher. The interaction took place in the classroom while other children were engaged in various worthwhile activities: some children were reading in the library corner, others were writing, listening to stories in the listening area, painting, drawing, playing in the post office (therefore speaking, listening, reading, writing and working with numbers), and so on. All of that required careful prior organization by the teacher. But it also enabled the teacher to engage Richard in a shared reading of *The Very Hungry Caterpillar* (Carle, 1969). This story was a popular one with the children in the classroom and had been read by the teacher to the class on more than one previous occasion. Perhaps for that reason the teacher did not read the story again with Richard. Instead Richard began, almost immediately, to read from the book.

Richard: I've got The Hungry Caterpillar.
Teacher: It is The Hungry Caterpillar, isn't it?
              Shall we read it together?
Richard: Yeah.
Teacher: Come on then.
                   In
Richard: In the
Teacher/Richard (T/R)   [reading alongside each other: the first named indicates who might be leading the reading]
                   light
Richard: of the moon
                   the – the (a)
T/R: little
Richard: egg
Teacher: Yes.
Richard: lay on a leaf.
Teacher: Yes.
              It lay on a leaf, didn't it?
              Can you see the egg?
Richard: Yeah – Yeah.

Yeah but the other day I looked at the pictures and I thought it was a hole.

Teacher: Did you? [Laughs]

Without the prior reading of the book by the teacher to Richard the only introduction to the story was the brief comment on the title. Seen in isolation that would seem to be an inadequate introduction to the shared reading interaction. However, in the context of previous readings of the book by the teacher to the class and, as we shall see later, in the context of Richard having a copy of the book at home, perhaps the start was not inappropriate.

Notice, too, how Richard was not 'on trial'. He was not expected to read the book to the teacher, although very largely he did just that in the event. Instead, he was invited to 'read it together': there was to be a genuine sharing of the story. This might seem like a very small point, but the invitation to read together (providing it is followed by episodes which indicate the genuine nature of that invitation) can be important. It sets the scene for subsequent happenings and puts the reader at ease.

The reading gets under way with the teacher reading 'In', Richard reading 'In the', and the teacher leading Richard in a combined reading of the word 'light'. Furthermore, the simple miscue of the text word 'a' when Richard read 'the' received no teacher mediation. To do so would have been to distract Richard from the meanings of the story. And, of course, in other contexts Richard can read 'a', as he does so later in the sentence.

At first sight the transcription might give the impression of a very disjointed reading of the story. That was not the case in reality and, indeed, if you read through the transcript a few times you will begin to get a feel for the flow of the interaction. The teacher and Richard were sharing the reading of the story and each was moving to the foreground or background as reader depending upon Richard's ability to take on, or not take on, the prominent role.

At the end of the first page of reading the teacher and Richard engaged in a very brief discussion about the events of the story. So the natural break created by turning from one page to another was used to encourage Richard's involvement with the story. But the discussion was brief because the reading of the book was the major emphasis. The teacher therefore encouraged Richard to restart the reading, this time with the teacher just behind and in support of that reading.

Teacher: Come on then.
R/T: One
Richard: summer (Sunday)

My mum's got The Hungry Caterpillar – it's – my mum's got – I've got that book like you.

One summer's(Sunday) day(morning) the warm sun came out(up) and – pop! – //

Eh.

T/R: out
Richard: of the egg

a very(came)

Teacher: came
Richard: came a tiny and very hungry caterpillar.
Teacher: It did come up didn't it one morning, yes.

On this page of reading Richard demonstrated a mix of emergent reading and some conventional reading where the print, or his memory of the story, determined his reading. The pictures in the book may have led Richard to read 'One summer's day' rather than the text of 'One Sunday morning'. The teacher accepted that reading and supported him through the rest of the page. However, the teacher comment at the end of the page served to confirm Richard's reading ('It did come up didn't it') but also informed him about the text, as the sentence was completed with 'one morning'.

Once again during this page of reading the teacher and Richard moved into and out of the role of lead reader. Therefore, as Richard hesitated in his reading after 'the warm sun came out(up) and – pop! – // Eh', the teacher waited, then led Richard back into the reading with the word 'out' before dropping away to let Richard continue on his own. The teacher also provided some support following Richard's false start of 'a very' for 'came'.

At the start of the next page the teacher invited Richard back in to lead the reading.

Teacher: What did he start to do?
Richard: He looked(started)
Teacher: No.
Richard: He starts(started)
Teacher: Yes.

He started

Richard: to look for (some) food.
Teacher: He did.

He started to look for some food.

That page from the book contained just one short sentence and the teacher attempted to set the scene for the reading by asking 'What did he start to do?'. Richard, however, used the teacher's question to bypass 'started' and to tell about how the caterpillar 'looked'. The teacher might have let Richard carry on reading but on this occasion a soft 'no' (Smith, 1971) was given to inform Richard that his prediction did not conform to the text. This support enabled Richard to get back on track and he read 'He starts'. The teacher confirmed that reading but also informed about the actual wording of the text, 'Yes. He started'.

Finally, at the end of the page the teacher indicated to Richard that he was progressing well with his reading by confirming the actions of the caterpillar: 'He did.' Then the teacher emphasized the appropriateness of Richard's reading by modelling the complete sentence 'He started to look for some food.' before they moved on to read the next page.

Teacher:	Yes.
Richard:	On Monday
	he ate through
	one apple.
	But he was still
	hungry.
Teacher:	He was, wasn't he?
Richard:	On Tuesday
	he ate through
	two peppers(pears) //
Teacher:	They do look a bit like peppers.
	And they do begin with a 'p'.
	But they might be something else, do you think?
Richard:	pineapples – eh –
Teacher:	Do you think they're pears?
Richard:	Yeah.
T/R:	two pears,
Richard:	Eh.
	but he was
	still hungry.
Teacher:	He was still hungry, wasn't he?
Richard:	I saw – I saw on Dennis the cartoon he was making orange drinks with orange pears.
Teacher:	Was he?
Richard:	Yeah. Yeah, but Dennis's friend was a girl and they said – eh – then Dennis and the girl were doing pounds(?).
	Then Dennis said look at the pounds(?). Then he went phew – phew – and he was out of breath.
Teacher:	Was he?

Richard was able to read the first of the diary pages about the caterpillar in a conventional manner and also with expression and intonation. In part, that was because the sequence of writing about the caterpillar from Monday to Friday has a rhythm which children find especially appealing. In particular, the 'But he was still hungry.' is a sentence which all the children in the class had enjoyed. And it was a part of the story which the teacher, during story readings in the classroom, had encouraged the children to read in chorus. Therefore, when Richard came to that part of the story he was well prepared to provide a conventional reading.

On the Tuesday page Richard produced the miscue of 'peppers' (pears). He then hesitated (//), presumably because he recognized that the word that he had given did not match what he could see on the page. The teacher agreed that the illustrations did suggest that they might be peppers ('They do look a bit like peppers.') but also that the letter/sound at the start of each word was similar ('And they do begin with a p'). (The teacher does highlight letters and/or sounds when it seems appropriate to do so.) Perhaps using that guidance from the teacher, Richard then suggested 'pineapples' but his subsequent 'Eh' indicated that he was not happy with that response. At that point the teacher, not wanting to be diverted from the story for too long, suggested 'Do you think they're pears?', which enabled Richard to get back to the reading of the remainder of the page.

For whatever reason, when Richard completed the page, some connection was made in his mind to a television programme that he had seen. Richard then produced a monologue about the events which he was able to recall. The teacher listened to his contribution, demonstrating an acceptance of his viewpoint and indicating a genuine sharing in the interaction, then encouraged a return to the story.

Teacher: So what did the caterpillar do on Wednesday?
Richard: On Wednesday
            he ate through
            three plums,
            but he was still
            hungry.
Teacher: He was still hungry.
Richard: On Saturday (Thursday)
Teacher: Well what comes after Wednesday?
            On
Richard: Thursday
            he ate through
      one – two – three –
            four strawberries,

	but he was still
	hungry.
Teacher:	He was still hungry.
Richard:	On Friday
	he ate through
	five oranges,
	but he was still
	hungry.
Teacher:	He was still hungry!
	So then what?
Richard:	On Saturday
	he ate through
	one (piece of)
	chocolate
Teacher:	one piece
Richard:	of
	(chocolate) cake,
Teacher:	Yes.
	chocolate cake,
Richard:	one ice-cream (cone),
	one pepper(pickle),
T/R:	one pickle,
Richard:	one slice of salami(Swiss) cheese,
Teacher:	Swiss cheese,
Richard:	Swiss cheese,
	one slice of salami,
	one lollipop,
	one cheese(piece) – one
T/R:	one piece of
Richard:	cherry cake – pie,
	one sausage roll,
	one cupcake – cupcake,
Teacher:	and
Richard:	one slice of salami(watermelon)
Teacher:	one slice
Richard:	of watermelon.

On the Wednesday, Thursday and Friday pages the repetition and rhythm of the story enabled Richard to produce a relatively convention-al reading of the book, albeit that part of that reading 'But he was still hungry' might have been encouraged by his memory of the story pattern rather than a close attention to the print. Nevertheless, he was enabled to behave like a reader and to enjoy the reading. The only support he required at that stage was over the day of the week, 'Saturday' (Thursday).

However, the rhythm of the story changes somewhat when the Saturday page is reached. The illustrations are helpful to the young reader but the writing is more complex. The teacher therefore had to provide more support to enable the reading flow to be maintained. On occasions that support was to read alongside Richard and at other times it was to provide some words. Both of those strategies were helpful in facilitating Richard's reading.

Teacher: Then what happened?
Richard: That morning(night) he had a tummy(stomach) ache!
Teacher: He did have a tummy ache.
Why do you think he had a tummy ache?
Richard: Because he ate too many foods.
Teacher: He did, didn't he?
Right.
The next
Richard: The next day was Sunday
Teacher: again.
Richard: He – The caterpillar eated(ate) through one nice green leaf,
T/R: nice green
Richard: leaf
and that made him(and after that he felt) much better.
Teacher: Why do you think it made him much better?
Richard: 'Cos that's – that's what caterpillars eat. 'Cos that's what food caterpillars eat.
Teacher: It is the food that caterpillars eat.
And then what happened?
R/T: Now
T/R: he
R/T: wasn't
Richard: hungry caterpillar any more –
and he wasn't a little caterpillar any more.
Teacher: No, he wasn't.
Richard: He was a big fat caterpillar.
Teacher: He was a fat caterpillar.

Richard's miscues – 'That morning(night) he had a tummy(stomach) ache.' did not dramatically alter the meaning of the story so the teacher just confirmed the reading, although not the 'morning' for 'night'. Of course, it will be the teacher's knowledge of the reader that will influence the nature of the responses and the extent of the teacher support. All the time the teacher will be considering how best to guide the reader along the road towards independent reading, and then taking what seems to be the most appropriate action.

During this interaction Richard was demonstrating his growth in reading as well as his continuing development as an oral language user: 'The caterpillar eated(ate) through . . . '. And with this story Richard was able to learn not only about stories, reading and language but also, in this case, about the natural sciences: 'Cos that's what food caterpillars eat'.

In the final section of that part of his reading, 'Now he wasn't hungry any more', Richard required support. It was interesting to note how he and his teacher were able to work and read together with first Richard in the lead, then the teacher, and then Richard again. There was a real sharing, with the teacher in support, and facilitating Richard's reading, but always ready to move back and allow Richard to lead whenever he was able to do so.

Teacher: And what did he do?
Richard: He built a
T/R: small
Richard: house, called a cocoon,
T/R: around
Richard: himself. He
T/R: stayed
Richard: inside for
                more than two weeks.
                He nibbled a little hole out(in)
Teacher: in
Richard: in the
Teacher: cocoon,
Richard: pushed his way out
Teacher: and
                What?
Richard: he was a beautiful butterfly!
Teacher: he was a beautiful butterfly.
                Wasn't he?
Richard: I saw on television a cocoon and a butterfly nibbled a little hole
                and pushed his way out.
                But he was different colours.
Teacher: Was he different colours?
                And you saw that on television?
Richard: Yeah, I saw that butterfly on television.

Teacher:	And you enjoyed that?
Richard:	And I saw – I saw a creature that eats caterpillars.
Teacher:	Who eats caterpillars?
Richard:	Some – sometimes beetles do.
Teacher:	Mmh.
Richard:	And sometimes some spiders do.
Teacher:	They do.
	Well you have read beautifully, haven't you?
	Well done Richard.

In this final part of the interaction Richard's reading of 'He built a small house called a cocoon' might suggest that he did indeed have a knowledge of the story before starting to read with his teacher. And he was able to extend that knowledge with a link from the text to his own experiences 'I saw on television a cocoon and a butterfly nibbled a little hole and pushed his way out.' Furthermore, that comment from Richard reinforced the view of the interaction being a real sharing; he was able to initiate part of the discussion and the teacher followed him in that initiation before some final words of encouragement from the teacher brought the interaction to an end.

The interaction that we have explored does not provide a simple example of the teacher reading and the child retelling, the teacher reading and the child providing an emergent reading, the teacher and child reading together, or the child producing a conventional reading. Instead, it was a shared reading which contained a mixture of most of these forms of interaction. In some respects it was useful to have that variety all in one interaction because it demonstrates that although a stated sequence can be helpful as a guide to what might be expected it does not provide a complete or a fully accurate picture of what might occur when an individual child reads with a teacher.

Nevertheless, what this interaction did demonstrate was a shared reading in which there was a genuine sharing and collaboration taking place. Although close analysis of the transcript might suggest a number of points where the teacher could have responded more helpfully, that has to be seen in the context of a teacher who has to make decisions on the spot not all of which the teacher, on reflection, might want to repeat. The teacher was attempting to respond to and work with the needs of the young reader. And the overall impression was that of a young reader being encouraged, guided, supported and facilitated towards independent reading.

Shared reading with real books is an important part of a real books approach. However, the view of Donaldson (1989) that other help has to be provided to encourage children towards literacy would receive substantial support. Goodman (1986) debated a range of activities which might be of help to children's reading development. And this book takes up that view and suggests that more is indeed required, and is utilized in reality, by teachers working within a real books approach. Indeed, some of those activities might precede, or at least run alongside, shared reading. Nevertheless, because real books and shared reading is how the approach is often seen it seemed to be important to start there before considering other aspects.

Of those other aspects, home–school links are important and, indeed, sometimes are linked very directly with shared reading. It might, therefore, be appropriate to consider those home–school links in the next chapter.

CHAPTER 4

Home–school links

When children first enter school at five years of age they have accumulated already a vast fund of knowledge. Through interactions with their parents, other significant adults, and perhaps brothers and sisters they will have been learning a range of social skills, physical skills and, most importantly, to understand and use language. Schools will want to build upon those foundations, but to do so without the collaboration of the home would not seem to be sensible or appropriate.

Davis and Stubbs (1988) suggested a connection between the establishment of those home–school links and shared reading within a real books approach. They did so for two main reasons. First, there was the recognition of the learning which the parents had encouraged during the first five years of the child's life. And there was the evidence which suggests that maintaining and developing that parental involvement during the school years can be beneficial to the child. Second, there was the difficulty of providing regular and frequent worthwhile shared readings within large classes. Both of these areas require some consideration. A major influence in the development of more positive home–school links was the publication of the Plowden Report (DES, 1967). That report on primary schools in England emphasized the influence of parental attitudes on educational performance.

It suggested that a strengthening of parental encouragement might serve to produce better educational performances in school. Looked at now, a quarter of a century on from the first publication of that influential report, the recommendations to develop home–school links seem relatively simple and restrained. Such suggestions were made as: a regular system for the headteacher and the classteacher to meet parents before the child enters school; arrangements for open days to enable parents to attend and for more formal private talks, preferably twice a year; booklets produced for the parents to describe the school; written reports on the children and an opportunity for the child's work to be seen by the parent; and special efforts to be made to contact those parents who do not visit the school. But there were also suggestions to involve the parents in the work of the school. In the area of literacy development there were suggestions of ways in which the parents might help, 'such as by reading to them and hearing them read' (DES, 1967, p.38). Those two key features of reading a story to the child and hearing the child read (akin to a shared reading) have subsequently been seen as crucial aspects which can support children in their reading development.

Research findings were also being published which added weight to the Plowden view which emphasized the home–school link and, in particular, parental involvement and encouragement. An intensive study by Clark (1976) of thirty-two children who were already reading fluently by the time they started school at five years of age, provided some evidence. The children came from a variety of home backgrounds and their parents had a wide range of educational experiences. However, the children did appear to have the advantage of an 'interested adult who talked to and listened to them' (p.102). Furthermore, they had belonged to libraries from an early age and were encouraged towards reading materials by their mothers, who were themselves avid readers. But few of the parents consciously set out to teach their children in a systematic way. Instead, there was 'an interested adult with time to devote to them at the stage when they were interested in reading – either to read to them, talk with them, or answer their questions' (p.102). It would seem, therefore, that rather than learning from direct teaching the children had benefited from having adults who encouraged their interest in reading, guided them towards appropriate materials and supported them in their attempts to understand about reading. So the attitude of the parent towards reading, the involvement of the parent, with the child, in literacy events and the encouragement of the child by the parent might be regarded as the important features of support for the child.

But if schools devote time and resources to developing a link with the home and encouraging parents to collaborate in children's reading development, would that have beneficial results? Two major and influential studies, the Haringey Project (Hewison and Tizard, 1980) and the Bellfield Reading Project (Jackson and Hannon, 1981), suggested it would.

Jenny Hewison had studied the reading attainment of seven- and eight-year-old-children in a working-class area of Dagenham. She considered that evidence alongside the details of the supportive home background that encouraged reading development. From that analysis she concluded that whether or not the mother heard the child read on a regular basis was the factor in the children's home background which was most strongly linked to reading attainment. The Haringey Project was designed to test such a view in an area where English was not the mother tongue for all the children.

In the Haringey Project the six- and seven-year-old children from six infant schools were divided into three groups. The first of these groups served as a control and continued with their normal school programme. The second were given additional help with their reading, in small groups, from a remedial teacher. In the third group parental involvement with reading was encouraged. So the children took home books to read to their parents two to three times a week. Furthermore, report cards were used to structure the reading and to allow comments to be made on the progress. After two years of the study it was found that the children in the reading-at-home group had made significant gains over the other children. However, not all of these gains had been retained one year after the project had been completed. But such evidence merely confirms the need not only to set up and develop such teacher–parent collaborations but also to maintain the links over the long term.

In the Bellfield Reading Project there was once again an emphasis upon the parents hearing their children read at home. In this project parents were encouraged to hear their child read for a few minutes five days a week. However, such projects do require careful planning and subsequent organization. Thus before this project was begun with the five-year-old children in the infant classes the structures of the scheme had to be set up. An evening meeting was organized for the parents to explain the scheme, and a list of do's and don'ts was developed to provide initial guidance for the parents in their support of the children. Once the scheme commenced a comment card was used to maintain and develop the links and make suggestions for the shared readings, and there were regular home visits made mainly by the project co-ordinator. The outcome of such careful planning and subsequent organization was that both parents and teachers were convinced that the scheme was beneficial.

Because of the apparent success of such reading-at-home several subsequent projects have emphasized reading at home with parental involvement. Bloom (1987) provided details of some of these projects and also emphasized the preparation for partnership with parents whether in the context of home reading or of support in the classroom from parents. Certainly there is now widespread agreement about the benefits to be gained from parental involvement in reading. For instance, the House of Commons Education, Science and Arts Committee (ESAC, 1991, p.xi) concluded that 'it would be hard to overstate the value of the active involvement of parents in "paired reading" and other activities'. Thus, there are very good reasons for establishing, maintaining and developing home–school links and parental involvement in shared reading at home.

However, Davis and Stubbs (1988) also argued for the encouragement of shared reading at home for more pragmatic reasons. Quite simply, they suggested that providing regular and frequent worthwhile shared reading interactions in large classes was difficult. The emphasis here is upon the quality of the interaction. And it is difficult, though not impossible, to provide worthwhile interactions. In Chapter 3 the example of Richard and his teacher reading together suggested that many teachers do organize and manage their classrooms so that worthwhile one-to-one interactions, such as shared reading, can take place.

Donaldson (1989, p.14) also argued that sustained one-to-one contact will be hard to achieve because 'real books have to be used by real teachers in real classrooms, where the class is likely to contain around thirty very real children'. She concluded that, although there will be a place for shared reading in the classroom, other literacy activities are also required. Nevertheless, the emphasis here upon the difficulty of maintaining, in all cases, a worthwhile shared reading does indicate the need for shared readings at home to support those occurring in school.

However, Tizard and Hughes (1984) warned that such interactions at home (they were actually debating interactions where the parent did most if not all of the reading, which they referred to as 'story reading', 'story time' or 'reading sessions') 'were rarely the cosy, idyllic occasions traditionally portrayed'. Tizard and Hughes did provide examples of interactions where the children questioned their parent, made comments about the text or made text-to-life connections and all of those features might be viewed positively. Nevertheless, the more negative comment that they made about many interactions serves to re-emphasize the importance of providing support and guidance for parents engaged in shared readings at home or school.

Communications with parents

Most schools that develop a home–school link for the purpose of involving the parents in shared readings with their children soon find that parents will seek guidance. Despite the fact that many parents will have been sharing books with their children in a natural and sensible manner up to the point of entry into school, that confidence is often replaced by uncertainty when their children start school. For that reason, and to guide other parents who may not have had literacy as a priority, schools produce sheets (Jackson and Hannon, 1981), booklets (Waterland, 1988; Burman, 1990b) and leaflets (Davis and Stubbs, 1988) about the process of shared reading.

But such written communications with the parents have to be considered carefully. And an important starting point for that consideration is the language that will be used: the use of educational jargon may not be helpful. Waterland (1988, p.61) gives the example of one school's booklet of advice for parents which included the suggestion: 'other useful methods you might like to use are syllabification and mnemonics'. It is doubtful whether such comments would create the right sort of invitation to a genuine collaboration for the benefit of the child. The notes sent to parents have to be written in such a way that they can be understood readily, have a positive and welcoming tone and do suggest that a geniune collaboration is sought. Many of the booklets now sent to parents are attractive and frequently contain illustrations, sometimes drawn by the children.

However, these communications will also be attempting to convey important messages about shared readings for those parents who feel that they need guidance or reassurance. The communications, therefore, whatever format they take, will attempt to cover the important issues of books, settings, enjoyment, preparation, sequence, the role of the listener, and praise:

Books:	Your child may want to read favourite stories time and time again. That's fine.
	Encourage a wide variety of reading material such as story books, information books, T.V. adverts and programme news, cereal packets and newspapers.
Setting:	Find a quiet place away from the television.
	Sit close together so that you can both see the print and the pictures.
Enjoyment:	Make sure that the atmosphere is happy and relaxed
	Remember that you want your child to enjoy the shared readings.
	Happy reading!
Preparation:	Look at the title and the pictures and talk about them.
	Try to guess what the story is about.
Sequence:	Read the story to your child.
	Let him/her talk about the story afterwards, or retell it in his/her own words.
	Later your child will want to join in the reading by saying some of the words.
	When your child is ready he/she will want to read the story to you after your reading.
Role of the listener:	When your child reads it won't be word perfect.
	Don't worry at this stage if the reader says 'house' for 'home' if it makes sense.

If it doesn't make sense:
1. Wait and see if the child will correct it.
2. Try starting the sentence again and see if that helps.
3. Suggest having another try at the word.
4. Suggest looking at the first letter of the word.
5. Tell the child the word.

Praise: Praise all your child's attempts, whether it is reading one or two words or phrases, reading from memory or making up his/her own story from the illustrations.

Praise and smile.

Of course, it is not suggested that the notes above are in a format to be sent to parents. They are comments taken from a range of booklets and demonstrate the kinds of issue that need to be considered for inclusion in a written communication to parents. But in each school there will need to be a debate about the length of the note, the extent of a written introduction, the inclusion of illustrations and the role of meetings and home visits to explain and expand upon the written communication. Only then will the school be able to determine the most appropriate note which best communicates the nature of the shared readings or other parental involvement.

Once the shared readings are linked between home and school it may be important to create a more regular communication between the teacher and the parent. Many schools find that a home-reading notebook (Burman, 1990b), 'What do you think book' (Heath, 1985), or some similar form of comment card can be used to encourage a working together. Of course, this process can be somewhat time-consuming, especially for the teacher with a large class. However, as Davis and Stubbs (1988) suggested, the comments do not need to be too comprehensive but they can help develop a good working relationship. Here is an example of a shared reading comment card for Richard:

Teacher: We talked about *The Very Hungry Caterpillar*. Can you read it to Richard?
Parent: I enjoyed this book and Richard did too.
Teacher: Very Hungry Caterpillar again, Richard is getting to know the story.
Parent: He loved it and he joined in with 'But he was still hungry' on each page.
Teacher: Richard won't let go of The Very Hungry Caterpillar, hope you are still enjoying it.
Parent: Yes it's lovely and Richard is reading more of it now.

With a comment card moving from the school to the home and back again both teacher and parent are aware of what the other is doing. Notice how the messages that the teacher sends to the parent are reinforcing the ideas of shared reading ('We talked about *The Very Hungry Caterpillar*'). Preparation in which the adult and the learner talk about the book is an important part of reading (Meek, 1988, provided a clear example of that preparation in her discussion of Ben, a young reader, sharing *Rosie's Walk* with her). The teacher asks 'Can you read it to Richard?' because part of the sequence is that we read first before the child can be expected to read the story back to us. Returning to familiar stories is to be expected ('Richard is getting to know the story') and is beneficial since memory and expectation can play an important part in the learning to read process. But the explanations for the comments do not have to be made. They become part of the parent's view of shared reading as the short and simple messages are sent to home on a regular basis.

Shared reading is an important part of the real books approach. And involving parents in these one-to-one interactions ensures that children get more opportunities to learn about reading and to learn to read. But, important as the home–school link undoubtedly is, teachers working with a real books approach would not assume that real books, shared reading and parental involvement are the end of the story. The organization and management of the classroom for a range of literacy activities are also very important. The next chapter will, therefore, consider the overall policy of the school, and organization and management within the classroom.

CHAPTER 5

School and classroom organization

The HMI report on *The Teaching and Learning of Reading in Primary Schools* (HMI, 1990) concluded, as might be expected, that effective leadership and a clear school policy had a major influence on the quality of classroom teaching and the reading standards achieved. But there is more to it than that. Effective leadership from both the headteacher and the language co-ordinator is based upon their being knowledgeable about reading and communicating that knowledge and enthusiasm to the staff and the parents. As Smith (1978) argued, teachers need to know about reading in general and children in particular in order to help them in their decision-making in the classroom. Knowing is important, but so is the enthusiasm. Southgate (1968) referred to 'reading drive' as being a crucial part of the formula that helps children become readers. That drive or enthusiasm from the teacher is an important part of the message that is conveyed to the learners.

Knowing about reading and enthusiasm for reading are an important basis for providing a clear school policy. That school policy has to be developed as part of a consultative process with all of the staff. In that way all the staff are involved in and understand the policy. Of course, any policy has to act as a framework which allows for flexibility as individual teachers bring their professional strengths and experience to work within the framework of the policy. Nevertheless, the policy is implemented in a more coherent manner when all the staff have been involved in its development. And the policy is best maintained and developed where the headteacher remains in close contact with the teachers, visits the classes regularly and shares books with the children (HMI, 1990).

It is crucial to think of maintaining and developing the school policy, because that keeps the important issue of reading development in the forefront of all the teacher's thinking, but also because it serves as a reminder during a period of major changes in primary schools that the emphasis upon other areas of the curriculum cannot be at the expense of the centrally important teaching of reading.

Adopting and developing a real books approach to literacy development requires, ideally, a debate in the staffroom leading to a school policy. It needs such a debate and policy in order to ensure that the full implications of a real books approach are appreciated. The danger exists otherwise of some strange and simplistic view of the approach being adopted where, as Cowland (1991) noted, the school simply throws away the reading schemes and starts using real books. This would entirely miss the point that the classroom organization for reading and the teaching offered by the teacher have to be considered in some detail. Indeed, there is a need to review every aspect of the teaching of reading when a real books approach is adopted (Coles, 1990). And that is the view taken in this book, which does explore a whole range of important issues that need to be considered. But for the moment we should examine, in this chapter, some of the important aspects related directly to the organization of the classroom.

Classroom organization

The first part of classroom organization that requires attention is that of the physical arrangement of the furniture. It is important that the classroom is arranged in a manner that facilitates individual or one-to-one interactions, group activities and the possibility of whole-class work whenever that is desirable. Typically, therefore, the class will have children's tables grouped to take four to six children, a number of single chairs and perhaps tables for individual work, and a large area (the rug, mat, or carpet) where the whole class can assemble. Cambourne (1988), Morrow (1989) and Burman (1990a) each provide plans of such classrooms where these principles are in operation. And these arrangements allow, even encourage, one-to-one shared readings, group work on a theme, the shared reading of a big book, or story reading by the teacher to the whole class.

Such an arrangement suggests movement and interaction and these are, indeed, part of the classroom activity which is organized for a real books approach. The movement is needed so that the children can acquire materials, move from one activity to another, consult charts and lists around the room, and access dictionaries or information books from time to time. And the interactions are encouraged so that the learners can support each other in their learning. The arrangement also makes it possible for the teacher to move around the room to encourage the kinds of interaction that are most constructive, or to move to a group engaged on writing and to support that writing for a period of time.

But, of course, the furniture is also arranged so that a number of corners or centres can be provided. So storage cupboards or trolleys and partitions are used to create a listening area, a library corner, and a writing centre. The first of these provides the opportunity for one or more children to listen, with headphones, to recorded stories and to follow these stories with the book in front of them. And the recordings do not have to be commercially produced ones. Indeed, children will take a great delight in hearing their own classteacher reading to them from the tape recorder. The listening area gives children the chance to hear one of their favourite stories frequently and to repeat that experience more frequently than would be possible with the busy teacher on a one-to-one basis or during storytime.

The library corner is a basic part of most early years classrooms. HMI (1990) reported that almost all such classrooms had reading areas. And for the reception class and years 1 and 2 they were usually carpeted, had bookshelves and often comfortable seating. However, the value of the areas for reading appeared to depend upon how well they were organized and maintained, and, in particular, the extent to which the children were involved in the running of the library corner. For a classroom in which a real books approach is being adopted the library corner is a central feature so that the key aspects which were noted by the HMI would be apparent. However, the teacher would be aimimg to achieve far more because the library corner should be acting as a magnet, attracting children to books.

Therefore, considerable care needs to go into the provision of the library corner. To think of such an area as a corner of the room where two walls provide the boundaries and where a few bookshelves, carpet and books turn it into a library corner is to underplay the value of the area. The comprehensive debate provided by Morrow (1989) indicated many of the aspects which need to be considered. The starting point is obviously in the planning of the area. The library corner needs to be planned with the children in mind and made visually attractive. Posters should be at the children's eye level, and the furniture, whether it be the shelves, chairs, tables or private nooks (made from large boxes with parts cut away for safety) should all be appropriate to the children. The visual attractiveness invites the children to enter but the walls, partitions, and shelves provide a physical boundary and privacy for the users. The children's comfort is enhanced by the use of carpets, soft chairs, sofa and/or bean bags. With a restricted area available for the library corner not all the children can or need to be accommodated at one time. Four to six children at any one time might be reasonable.

The books might need to be displayed using two different kinds of bookshelf. Many of the books will need to be shelved with only the spines showing. That might not be considered ideal, but if there are sufficient books for all the children in the class, perhaps five to eight per child, then some will need to be shelved in that manner. Others can be displayed with the covers showing, and changed on a regular basis. And there will be posters of books or of the characters of books on the pinboards, perhaps even stuffed toys related to some of the more popular stories on the shelves or larger partitions.

But all of that is designed to attract the children to the story books, nursery rhymes, fairy tales, picture books, poetry books, reference books, and so on. A substantial variety of books, probably dominated by story books, needs to be made available. And the children should be involved in some of the planning – Which books? What rules? – and the maintainence of the library corner When to change the displayed books? Whose turn to keep it tidy? That involvement helps the children learn about books, authors and referencing systems. It also encourages them to care for the books in their own library.

In addition to having the opportunity to listen to a story in the listening area or to read a book in the library corner the children should also be able to write at the writing centre which has been organized by the teacher. Part of that organization would be to ensure that there were various materials in sufficient quantities for the children to use. Pencils, coloured pencils, crayons, felt-tipped pens and chalks with chalkboards should be made available. Then a wide variety of paper, lined and unlined, in different colours, sizes and shapes should also be provided. Different writing tools or paper to write upon can be introduced from time to time to create a new interest. And the introduction of a typewriter or word processor will add to the excitement of writing. It might also be desirable to have scissors, glue and other such materials available so that the children can produce cards, posters and books.

The variety of materials will, in part, make the area an attractive one for the children. However, adding to the centre a message board or notice board for use by the teacher and the children will add to the attraction (Morrow, 1989). At the writing centre the children can be encouraged to write lists, messages, greetings cards, letters, stories or poems, produce signs and directions and write about personal events and experiences. However, this writing, like any other, has to have a purpose and an audience. Sheila Taylor (SCDC, 1989), reporting upon her experience of developing a writing table (centre) in a reception class, indicated that having the children work in small groups where they could share their writing with others helped encourage the ideas of purpose and audience, as did writing letters and receiving replies, showing their writing to other classes, the headteacher and parents, sending cards to friends in school, and producing books for others to read.

The physical organization of the classroom and especially the provision of a listening area, library corner and writing centre will thus facilitate the children's literacy development. Of course, there will also be other areas in the classroom, so that mathematics, science, art and other subjects are catered for. These subjects can be linked in many ways to reading and writing. Indeed, the teacher would want to ensure that the other subject areas were being used in a positive way to develop literacy. These links between the subject areas and literacy are explored further in Chapter 10.

Another part of the classroom organization that should be developed by the teacher is that of displays and wall charts. Indeed, Cambourne (1988, p.101) wrote about the need to 'flood the room with useful wall charts'. The teacher would, therefore, want to ensure that there was an abundance of writing/print around the classroom, each being used for a particular purpose. Environmental and classroom print will be considered in Chapter 6.

So organizing the classroom for literacy activities is an important part of the teacher's role. But it does not end there. The teacher does not just acquire real books, organize the classroom and then leave the children to learn. The teacher also has to manage the literacy activities with care.

Classroom management

The teacher, having provided the organization, needs to ensure that it works. At a general level this requires the teacher to move around the classroom, checking on the activities of the children, supporting the children's learning, guiding and correcting where necessary, providing information, encouraging and praising. A real books classroom, just like any other classroom, requires the teacher to manage the activities in that classroom.

In particular, the teacher needs to ensure that adequate time is devoted to literacy activities and that they are not merely completed but that there is a quality to the activities and the interactions.

It seems almost too simplistic to say that in order to develop children's reading and writing the teacher needs to ensure that sufficient time is devoted to literacy activities. Yet Harris (1979) found it important to remind us that the single most important characteristic of successful reading instruction was the amount of time spent on reading. More recently, the HMI (1990) recognized that with the time and energy that teachers were devoting to other National Curriculum subjects there was a need to ensure that the teaching of reading still received the attention (time) needed for it to be effective. The same would be true for writing.

So how might the class be managed in order to ensure that sufficient time was being devoted to literacy? Cambourne (1988) described an organization of time in a primary school which he believed worked well. The first two hours of the school day were devoted to language. Those two hours were divided into four main components. First, about ten minutes were given to a whole-class focus. That whole-class focus might typically involve the teacher in reading to the class or writing in front of the class. Second, up to twenty-five minutes were devoted to sustained silent reading (SSR); this period might last no longer than ten minutes in the case of younger children who are not able to read in the conventional sense. Third, about an hour was devoted to activity time: children would be engaged with reading and writing, sometimes of their choosing and at other times on an activity provided by the teacher. Finally, the time was brought to a close with another whole-class period. Children could then report on their reading and writing, and listen to others.

Of course, other schools and/or classes may wish to manage the time differently. The story reading at the end of the school day is frequently noted (Trelease, 1984), and SSR immediately before or after the lunch break is often part of a school policy (Campbell, 1990a). Then, with the classroom organized for a wide variety of subjects and with various areas, centres and corners, the children can be engaged in literacy activites and other subjects throughout the rest of the day. However, within such an organization it is important for the teacher to ensure that each child not only listens to the story reading and takes part in SSR but also devotes substantial parts of the day to other reading and writing activities.

Furthermore, the quality of the interactions that take place between teacher and child have to be considered. Donaldson (1989) expressed her concern about the quality of the shared reading interactions in the classroom where large classes were the norm. Campbell (1988) noted that it was the nature and quality of the oral reading interaction as much as the time spent on it which was important. The teacher, therefore, needs to ensure that the classroom environment provides the framework for worthwhile interactions to take place. It is also important that the nature of the questions asked by the teacher and the extent and nature of the guidance given are such that they support the learner in his/her growth as a reader and writer.

So the teacher has been involved in the school debate about the language policy. And arising out of that framework develops a classroom organization. But that organization needs careful management in order to ensure that sufficient time is spent by each child on literacy activities and that those activities are of the highest quality and meet the needs of the child. As Cambourne (1988) argued, to the untrained eye the events in the classroom might appear to be disorganized, but that is because the teacher is not constantly standing in front of the class and teaching directly. However, it is quite inappropriate to think of the real books approach as being a non-teaching movement. As has been argued in this chapter, the teacher is very much engaged in the art of teaching and that is demonstrated by the attention to the organization and management of the classroom.

CHAPTER 6

Environmental and classroom print

In the previous chapter it was suggested that the teacher would want to pay attention to the displays and wall charts in the classroom. The teacher would want to use every possible opportunity to demonstrate the import-ance and value of print as a means of communication. However, the teach-er would also want to provide a link with the print in the environment external to the school. After all, the children will have been surrounded by that environmental print before starting school and in many instances will already have begun to make sense of some of it. Therefore, the teacher will need to ensure that much of the environmental print is brought into the classroom to be talked about and used by the children. Furthermore, the teacher will want to provide opportunities within the play activities of the classroom for the children to engage in reading and writing of that en-vironmental print in a meaningful way.

Each of the separate, but linked, features of environmental print and classroom print, together with reading and writing of the environmental print during classroom play, needs to be considered and developed by the classroom teacher. In doing so the teacher will be creating a high profile and status for literacy and will be providing the opportunity to engage in purposeful literacy acts, both of which Hall (1987) argued were critical if the emergence of literacy was to be continuous.

Environmental print

During their days before entering school children, in most societies, are surrounded by print. That environmental print, or 'embedded print' as Donaldson (1989) referred to it, is most typically seen within its own context. And because the print is contextualized, as when the words 'fish and chips' appear above a fish and chip shop (Hall, 1987) or the word 'cornflakes' on a packet of cornflakes, children are assisted in grasping the meaning of the print. Evidence to support such a view can be found in the case studies of children developing as readers and writers before school.

Baghban (1984) indicated that her daughter, Giti, could clearly distinguish print by the age of 20 months. For instance, Giti consistently identified the broad yellow 'M', for McDonald's, whether it stood alone, appeared in an advert or was on a cup. And a number of other shop logos were learnt and recognized in various contexts by the time she was two years of age. That understanding of logos extended to those used on various grocery items, so that Giti could collect items from the shelves in supermarkets when on shopping expeditions with her mother. Giti also responded to the appearance of logos and familiar items on television advertisements. She was learning about the communicative nature of print.

Laminack (1991) concluded that it was because children are naturally curious about their world that when they spot print in the environment they focus attention on it. And they attempt to create meanings for that print. Laminack's son, Zachary, at thirteen months, responded to a question about a 'Stop' road sign by indicating that it said 'Stop the truck'. So road signs provided an introduction to literacy, but logos, adverts, shopping products, TV programmes and commercials all became part of Zachary's reading repertoire. When confronted by new print, Zachary would make a logical connection from that which he already knew to that which was new and unknown. At times the specific response, provided by Zachary, might seem strange to adult ears. However, what was evident was that Zachary was using the available clues and his previous knowledge in order to respond to the print. It is important that adults try to detect the connections that the child is making and then support the child in his/her understanding of the environmental print. As Laminack noted, the child is aided greatly in coming to terms with the print in the environment if significant adults invite predictions with an emphasis upon meaning, then support and encourage the child's responses.

As might be expected, children demonstrate a literacy growth in their response to environmental print with age. However, that growth is not directly related to increasing years but rather is the product of encounters with environmental print supported by an adult (Harste *et al.*, 1984). Given such supported encounters, children will provide an increasingly specific response rather than a functional or categorical response to environmental print. Harste *et al.* provided an example of that development with children's responses to Crest toothpaste. A functional response might suggest 'toothbrush', the later categorical response would be 'toothpaste' and the subsequent specified response 'Crest'. But each of these responses is indicative of the child's attempts to make sense of the environmental print.

Although in Chapter 4 we concentrated upon shared readings

between the parent and the child, it might be that a school would also want to discuss with parents the importance of the learning that takes place during encounters with environmental print. In such a discussion the variety of meaningful print might be emphasized to include: T-shirt slogans and clothes labels; soft drink cans, crisp packets and other consumables with print on the container; road signs and notices in buildings; the abundance of print on the shelves in the supermarket; TV print, including commercials and programmes; newspapers, magazines and comics; telephone directories; and cook books. But, most importantly, it is not just that the children are surrounded by meaningful print but that they also see people using that print (Wray and Medwell, 1991). As Laminack (1991) noted, adults' demonstrations of the use of print for meaningful purposes will be observed by the children and subsequently tried out for themselves.

In the classroom the teacher adopting a real books approach will want to build upon these naturally occurring experiences with literacy. Collections of boxes, cartons, labels, newspapers, and so on, can be used to emphasize the importance of print to convey information, and the T-shirts worn by the children can be used to spot words and read messages (Burman, 1990a). The children can go for walks around the school to find print and to guess at what the various labels and signs mean. That can be extended to escorted walks in the neighbourhood of the school to look for environmental print and, as Goodman (1986) suggested, to ask 'Why is the print there?' and 'What does it say?'

In part, therefore, children go out of the classroom to consider the richness and complexity of environmental print, but that print is also brought into the classroom to be displayed and used. But the teacher will want to go beyond that and develop a range of meaningful examples of classroom print.

Classroom print

The aim of the teacher will be to create a print-rich environment in the classroom as part of the early literacy curriculum (Hudson, 1988). This might serve as a contrast to some early years classrooms where colourful children's paintings, posters, and giant collages of characters and scenes from stories might seem to have led to the banishment of print from the classroom (Wray and Medwell, 1991). Which is not to say that the colourful artistic work should be excluded from the classroom but that a balance needs to be reached where, in addition to artistic displays, there is also an abundance of classroom print. As already mentioned, Cambourne (1988) emphasized this need by suggesting that when teachers organize the resources of the classroom they should flood the room with useful wall charts.

But it does have to be useful and serve a real communicative purpose. Donaldson (1989), for instance, argued that it is useful and functional to put a 'pencil' label on a drawer or box which contains pencils that are out of sight, but less useful simply to attach a 'chair' label to a chair.

But there will be a good deal of opportunity for the teacher to provide print in the classroom and for real purposes. Goodman (1986), Hall (1987) and Cambourne (1988) are among a number of whole language/emergent literacy (real books) writers who have listed suggestions for classroom print. Those suggestions include:

- *Attendance charts.* These are particularly important for the very young children who will, of course, be interested in their own name.
- *Message board.* In particular, this can be used to tell about important events that are to occur during that day.
- *Bulletin board.* This might be used to indicate future happenings and be separate from the message board in order that the children are not distracted from the daily notices.
- *Functional labels.* The labels on the various drawers, cupboards and equipment are important suppliers of information for the children so that they can be encouraged to work independently of the teacher as a supplier of pencils, paper and other materials.
- *Birthday chart.* This will not only indicate the timing of an important event for the child but also provide a number of sequences, such as the months of the year, days of the week, and cardinal numbers up to 31.
- *Weather chart.* The children can be given the responsibility for recording the weather on this wall chart. This activity brings together science, writing and reading.
- *Classroom rules and expectations.* The teacher will be able draw the children's attention to the written statements relating to classroom behaviour and activity. Frequently the children will want to add new ideas to this list. And their suggestions can often be draconian in nature!
- *Job responsibilities.* This will require changing on a frequent basis but it will serve as a reminder to the children of jobs to be completed and it will often form the basis of discussion among children.
- *Directions for activities.* Such a chart might serve two main purposes: first, to suggest and remind of possible activities for the day; and second, to serve as general guidance, indicating, for example, the number of children who can be at the listening area at any one time.
- *Record charts.* These can be developed and used by children to record work completed, books read or observations made.
- *Explanatory labels.* Displays and exhibits would have labels of explanation or amplification.
- *Children's written work.* This would be positioned so that it can be read by

other children in the classroom. In the library corner there might be summaries by the children of books that they had read.

- *Songs and poems.* These favourite songs and poems would be on large charts and sung or read together by the teacher and the children with some frequency.
- *References.* Lists of importance to the children, alphabetic frieze, dictionaries and other reference sources.

Of course, not all of these might be avialable in the classroom at any one time. The age and literacy development of the children might mean that one class would have an attendance chart to sign whereas later there might be, as Cambourne (1988) suggested, a chart of synonyms, metaphors, similes and problem words. But whatever charts there might be, to extend the classroom print beyond the books in the library corner, the teacher will have to ensure that there is a balance between teacher and child writing, that the labels, charts and writing are kept up to date and that fading print is replaced. But, most importantly, the teacher will have to recognize that all of that print is of little value if it is not in constant use and accompanied by discussion and reflection (Hall, 1987).

In addition to the use of environmental print and the provision of classroom print, the teacher will also want to ensure that there is ample use by children of environmental print during classroom play activities.

Literacy during classroom play

The play, role-play or home corner is a typical feature of the infant classroom. However, the area can be used to promote reading and writing by the adequate provision of the products and tools of literacy, as Wray and Medwell (1991) argued. They suggested that where the area was being used as small-scale replica of a home, complete with a model kitchen, there might in addition be newspapers, magazines, television and radio programme information; recipe books; instructions for working the various kitchen implements; telephone directories; books for the children to read for themselves; books to read to the doll or stuffed animals; bills and final demands; pens and pencils; note-pads, letter-pads and envelopes; a wipe-clean shopping list pad. All of these items serve to encourage the children to incorporate literacy activities into their play.

But the home corner does not have to remain solely as a replica of a home. For example, Wray and Medwell went on to note the literacy events that were observed when a group of four- and five-year-old children used the area as a pretend dentist's surgery. The children browsed through magazines while waiting their turn; consulted charts to diagnose the dental problems of 'patients'; used telephone directories when 'phoning' hospitals or neighbours; wrote prescriptions; and filled in appointment bookings. In their detailed study of the use of play activities to promote literacy, Morrow and Rand (1991) suggested that the home corner could be changed into any of the following:

- *Veterinarian's Office.* A waiting room would require magazines and the office would have books and posters about pets. There might also be office notices, prescription pads, records of the animals and numerous stuffed animals.
- *A Restaurant.* Menus, order-pads, posters with the day's specialities and a cash register (so linking to mathematics) would be needed in the re-arranged corner.
- *A Newspaper Office.* A telephone, writing-pads, a typewriter (possibly a computer) and information in the form of books, magazines and posters on sports, weather, travel and general news would all be helpful, plus examples of newspapers. Of course, once established this play activity can easily spill over into the classroom and the development of a class newspaper can occur.
- *A Supermarket or Grocery Shop.* This links particularly well with the environmental print outside the classroom as the children can bring into school food packets or cartons to place on the shelves with labels and prices.
- *A Post Office.* Paper, envelopes, address books, stamps and various forms provide the starting point. But a post box and a bag for delivering letters will encourage the writing of messages and the need to read the names on the envelopes.
- *A Petrol Station and Car Repair Shop.* Road maps, car magazines and manuals, together with numerous toy cars and a variety of car posters, can stimulate the organization of routes and bills for repairs.

This list can, of course, be extended and each teacher will observe the possibilities from the external environment of the school. However, two important principles need to be considered in all cases: first, that numerous and appropriate reading and writing materials need to be included in the redesigned home corner; and second, the teacher needs to suggest and demonstrate possible uses for the literacy materials by playing alongside the children briefly when the home corner is transformed.

So the use of environmental print can be encouraged by the play activities of the home corner. And that provides an important link to the rich and varied print environment beyond the school. It also confirms the emphasis placed upon print within the classroom. But none of that is instead of real books and shared readings. They are still a central feature of the classroom, as are other classroom interactions with books, and it is one of those classroom interactions, story reading by the teacher, to which we now turn.

CHAPTER 7

Story reading

This chapter could have appeared very much earlier in the book. After all, story reading, on a daily basis or even more frequently, is a starting point for many teachers as they attempt to encourage children's literacy development. And for a teacher following a real books approach it will be a very important part of the day as it is the means by which the teacher can introduce to the children a wide variety of story books.

The emphasis on story reading reflects also the way in which, in many homes, parents will spend time reading to their children on a regular basis. Laminack (1991) reported that he started to read books to his son when Zachary was just three months old. And he had been engaged in storytelling from an even earlier age with different stories told according to the context, whether being rocked to sleep or being fed. With such a background Zachary was well placed to develop as a reader, for the importance of story reading and the learning which can occur from such interactions are well documented.

Importance of story readings

On the basis of his experience with, and observations of, his son developing as a reader, Laminack suggested a number of strategies that might be employed in order to encourage beginning literacy. Among these suggestions was that of 'read aloud regularly'. Story reading, Laminack argued, gave an opportunity for a parent (or significant adult) to communicate to a child an appreciation of literature. More simply, Trelease (1984) suggested that children learn to enjoy reading by being read to, so much so that a child may request to have the same story repeated time and time again. In part, that will be because the child will feel secure with a repetition of a previous encounter. But it will also be because, with repeated readings, the child can make the book his/her own and begin to exert some control over the story. (Try changing even a single word of a well-known and well-loved story and see how quickly the child will intervene.)

There is, too, evidence from research projects to suggest that story readings exert a positive influence upon children's literacy development. The longitudinal Children Learning to Read project in Bristol, which Gordon Wells directed, led him to suggest that listening to stories and, in addition, taking part in discussions about those stories was significantly associated with children's subsequent literacy development (Wells, 1986). Evidence such as that led Teale (1984), in his survey of reading to young children, to conclude that story reading had numerous facilitative effects on literacy development.

However, although there is this evidence from case studies and longitudinal studies, there is occasionally evidence which conflicts with the prevailing view. The retrospective study by Torrey (1969) of a five-year-old, the third child in a family of five children, indicated that children can learn to read early without having been read to by parents. John's mother indicated that no one had read to him or taught him to read. However, he had learnt all the TV commercials by heart and was able to recite them as they appeared on the screen. And the earliest evidence of his reading was when he read the labels of cans in the kitchen. So although this study does raise a question about the absolute necessity of story readings to encourage reading development, it would appear to provide evidence to support the earlier views (see Chapter 6) of the importance of environmental print. Furthermore, for every study that raises such a question there are others which seem to confirm the importance of story reading. For instance, in her comprehensively documented account of reading stories to her daughter from two to five years of age, White (1984) demonstrated vividly the language and literacy growth that appeared to be associated with regular and frequent story readings at home.

Story reading at home would appear to be beneficial and, where necessary, might be encouraged within the context of home–school links. But what about at school? Can the teacher with a large class create the same kind of enjoyable atmosphere and interaction which will encourage literacy development? Wells (1986) suggested that for some children listening to a story with the whole class might be too impersonal. The teacher might, therefore, need to attempt to arrange for some children to have one-to-one story readings in the same way as many children would have had at home. This, too, was the view of White (1984), who believed that the task of reading to more than one child in an infant classroom would not provide the kind of experience that the child required. However, that need not be the case. If the teacher has attended to the details of classroom organization and management then it should be possible for the children to have an enjoyable experience and to gain from the reading to the whole class. Cambourne (1988) indicated that he had observed over the years teachers who read to the whole class. He made a number of positive statements about the children's enjoyment and involvement during such sessions. And others (Dombey, 1988, with an example from a nursery school; and Campbell, 1990a, with two examples from an infants' school) have provided transcriptions of story readings to indicate the way in which the children were learning from the experience.

Learning during story readings

In broad terms, it has already been suggested that children learn about the enjoyment of reading during story readings, and that these interactions provide a foundation for future literacy development. Story reading does so because it teaches children about books and how books work (Meek, 1984). Who can doubt that the child who has been read to regularly will do anything other than acquire an understanding of books and an interest in them? But, of course, that interest is aided by the parent, and subsequently the teacher, making a careful selection of the books to be read. And the selection is important because it not only stimulates the interest of the child but also encourages emotional, social and psychological development (Trelease, 1984) as the child becomes immersed in the characters, setting and plot of the stories. Such involvement with the stories also provides a source of play activities for the child, and White (1984) reported many occasions when her daughter, Carol, used a story to form the basis of her play.

But there are also some specific features that appear to be learnt during story readings, not because it is taught directly but because the demonstration of reading and the involvement of children in that reading ensures that learning takes place. At a simple level, they learn how to handle books so that front-to-back and left-to-right directionality becomes part of their awareness and understanding (Strickland and Morrow, 1989). They also learn about authorship and illustration (Meek, 1988), especially where the teacher comments upon these features as part of an introduction to a story reading.

Teale (1984) argued that an important feature of story reading was that it familiarized children with literary conventions. Thus children begin to develop an understanding of story structure or story grammar as they listen to a wide variety of stories. Their own attempts to retell, tell or write a story will demonstrate that developing knowledge of beginning, middle and end, character, setting and plot, and so on.

They will also be learning about language. In *Rosie's Walk*, for instance, there are the words 'across', 'around', 'through' and 'over' which are key to the flow of the story. Hearing them in the context of the story, not only will the children acquire a knowledge of these prepositions but they will also learn the nuances of the words. Additionally, as Dombey (1988) argued, children will acquire an understanding of new syntactic forms, new meanings and new ways of organizing discourse as well as new words when they listen to a variety of stories. Holdaway (1979) indicated that once children became aware of the pattern and structure of the sentences and discourse of a story they would be aided subsequently in their own reading of that book. Earlier we noted a simple example of this, where Richard was helped in his reading of *The Very Hungry Caterpillar* by the repetition and rhythm of 'But he was still hungry'.

In part, children will be gaining an enjoyment of reading and learning about story structure and language because of the power of stories. However, they will also be learning about these things because the teacher will have given careful thought to the nature of the story readings.

The nature of story readings

Perhaps the first comment to be made on the nature of story readings relates to the regular and frequent basis of these classroom literacy events. Especially in the early years, a daily reading would not be inappropriate; indeed, many teachers would argue that to read only once during the course of the school day may be to underplay the importance of story readings. Trelease (1984) suggested that a set time should be allocated for this activity; the mere fact of doing so indicates its importance. Often the end of the school day is used for this purpose, and that is suitable providing that adequate time is allocated, that the previous activity does not restrict the story reading, and that the story reading does not become a ritualized activity (that should not be the case in the classroom where stories/real books receive such a major emphasis). Other early years teachers find that the beginning of the school day is a good time for story reading, especially where the children might want to use the story as a basis for their play, art work or writing.

The teacher will, of course, have selected the book carefully and pre-read it so that the story reading can be one of thoughtful reading and enthusiasm. Trelease argued that teachers should not read stories they do not enjoy themselves as that lack of enjoyment might show through in the reading. And, of course, the prereading is essential in a book where the illustrations tell so much of the story, so that the teacher's knowledge of the story will enable him/her to combine the reading of the text with a showing of the pictures. That showing of the pictures, especially the front cover, may occur before the reading starts.

The structure of a story reading is often seen (see, for example, Campbell, 1990a; Mason *et al.*, 1989) as being composed of three parts. Each of those parts, before the reading, the reading itself, and after the reading, will contribute to the children's understanding of the particular story and of reading more generally. They need, therefore, to be given some thought by the teacher.

First, before the reading occurs, the teacher should show the children the cover of the book. Meek (1984, p.8) indicated in her interaction with Ben that the cover was a starting point before reading: 'First we looked at the cover and talked about the hen, the foxes, the bees, and the trees with apples and pears. Ben was the leader of the discussion.' Of course, in that instance the audience was of just one child and therefore the nature of the activity might be altered. Nevertheless, the principle remains that the cover can be shown and that this provides the basis for talk about the main characters in the story and perhaps the setting and some of the plot. However, the teacher will often want to go beyond that to talk about the author and the illustrator so that, as Meek indicated, the children begin to understand about authorship and audience. The discussion about the author becomes particularly important as the children begin to become knowledgeable about authors. Making connections between, for example, Pat Hutchins's books *Rosie's Walk* (1969) and *Goodnight Owl* (1973) often encourages children to look for other books by the same author.

During this discussion before the reading of the book, the teacher might also encourage the children to make some predictions about the story. After all, prediction of a text will be an important part of the reader's strategies when engaged upon an individual reading of a book. The teacher might also try to make text-to-life connections with the children so that they are able to contextualize the story within their own view of the world. Of course, not all of these elements will become part of each story reading. The teacher's knowledge of the children, their development as readers and their familiarity with the book, will assist the teacher in making decisions about the prereading of the story.

Once started on the reading of the book, the teacher will need to be prepared for the many comments and or questions that will be initiated by the children. That will be especially the case when the teacher is reading to younger children. The teacher is then faced with the difficult task of responding to those comments and questions but maintaining a flow to the story reading. But this can be achieved, and many teachers are able to create a balance between demonstrating an acceptance of the child's thoughts by responding to them and using the response as a means of returning to the story (see the examples in Campbell, 1990a).

At times during the reading the teacher might ask a question of the children or ask them to predict what might happen. However, it is important not to break the flow of the reading and many teachers will use the natural breaks in the story, often the turning of a page in stories for very young readers, to seek a response. Cambourne (1988) suggested that these teacher interruptions should be minimal and serve a special purpose such as to make the listeners aware of how texts are structured or to focus, for younger children, on an interesting word, but typically these interruptions are always followed by an immediate return to the story.

When the children are older the teacher may find that the stories can be read with few interruptions as the children internalize their thoughts and are content to comment and question after the story has been read. And the teachers can save their questions until after the reading.

When the story reading has been completed the children may wish to comment about the story or ask a question about it. Or the teacher might ask the children about the story, the characters, setting, or plot, and perhaps get the children to express a view of the story and their feelings towards it. However, as Trelease (1984) warned, we need to avoid turning the discussion into a quiz during which story interpretations are prised from the children. With the very young children a key aim is to encourage an enjoyment of books and to develop an enthusiasm for reading. Nevertheless, a discussion will often follow the story reading as a natural part of the session and the teacher will help the children make connections from the story to their own lives.

Story readings will be an important part of the day for a teacher following a real books approach because stories, meanings and discussion are seen to be such a central element in children's literacy development. However, there will also be other important literacy interactions in the classroom for the teacher to consider. The next chapter will explore these interactions.

CHAPTER 8

Classroom interactions with books

The teacher employing a real books approach will make frequent use of story readings with the class and shared readings with individuals. These two interactions are crucial and have already been debated in two earlier chapters. However, they are not the only interactions that will be used by the teacher in order to encourage the children's use and exploration of stories. Other interactions with the whole class, a group from the class, or an individual will also take place.

Shared readings with a big book, hearing a child read, sustained silent reading and using nursery rhymes and songs are all likely to be evident in the classroom at various times of the day. Many of these interactions are not unlike those of story reading and/or shared reading, but there may be changes in the groupings of the children and in the role of the teacher or child. What remains, however, is the importance of story, the guiding, supporting and facilitating role of the teacher and the involvement of the child as a meaning maker.

Shared reading with big books

There does appear to be a slight difference in the use of the term 'shared reading' between the UK, on the one hand, and Australia and New Zealand, on the other. In the UK shared reading is most typically seen as a teacher–child interaction (see, for example, Davis and Stubbs, 1988; Waterland, 1988) and thus is individually based. In Australia and New Zealand shared reading is more typically defined as a class or group activity with the use of a big book (Holdaway, 1979). Increasingly, however, many teachers are making use of both notions as they may serve somewhat different purposes. The one-to-one shared readings provide the opportunity for the teacher to guide, support and assess the individual child. The earlier example of Richard

Richard reading with his teacher demonstrated some of these benefits. However, shared reading with a big book allows the teacher to work with more children and can be employed usefully alongside the individual approach.

Holdaway (1979) provided a detailed account of the development and use of shared readings with big books. The starting point for that development was that there might be a disparity between the benefits of story reading at home and at school. Wells (1986) and White (1984), it will be recalled from Chapter 7, had expressed some concern about the experience a child would have during a class-based story reading. However, during a shared reading with a big book not only would the children be able to share and discuss the book with the teacher but they would also, as at home, be able to see the text. Shared reading with a big book might, therefore, be seen as a bridge between story reading and individual shared readings.

As in a story reading the teacher might instigate some discussion about the book before, during or after the reading. However, now, as the text can be seen by all the children in the class the teacher can use a pointer to follow the story. And pointing, especially for the youngest children, is crucial, Holdaway (1979) argued, because it provides the insight that print moves from left to right along the line, back and down. Furthermore, it demonstrates the one-to-one relationship between spoken and written words. Therefore, particularly for those children who may not have had a substantial number of story readings or involvement with books at home before arriving at school, the pointing may be of value.

On second and subsequent shared readings with a big book the children, now becoming familiar with the story, are likely to join in the reading. That will be particularly true of the repetitive and rhythmic sections of a book. The repetition of 'But he was still hungry' from *The Very Hungry Caterpillar* is just one obvious example of where children like to join in with the reading of a big book. Holdaway indicated that children could be encouraged to participate in shared reading by joining in on repetitive sections, suggesting obvious words or predicting possible outcomes. The children might also join in with a choral reading of the story alongside the teacher (Goodman, 1986). This variety of involvement is encouraged where favourite stories are reread. Furthermore, those rereadings can continue to the point where the children know the complete story. When that occurs the teacher is likely to note, as Holdaway did, that on occasions some children will come together as a spontaneous group to share a big book. In such an activity a child will model the role of the teacher pointing to the words and expecting participation from the other children in the group.

The shared reading of a big book need not be seen as single activity where one book is read and then the children disperse to other activities. In any one session a number of books, and poems, might be read. This would include some books that the children knew well, others with which they were becoming familiar, and perhaps one book introduced to them for the first time. After all, these books for the very young reader will be relatively short. Nevertheless, although the teacher will structure the session to include a number of books, the overall objective to provide an enjoyable experience of stories for all the children will remain. Holdaway (1979) argued that such an objective should not be sacrificed to any other purpose. And if the children do enjoy the stories then there is the possibility of getting them hooked on books with the growth in and understanding of language and literacy that will bring.

Hearing children read

The practice of hearing children read (Campbell, 1988) or listening to children reading (Arnold, 1982) has been a well-established classroom practice in infant classrooms in the UK for many years. And although there is a danger that the activity might, in some classes, have become a ritualized interaction in which the child is mainly assessed and most of the miscues are responded to by the teacher giving the word or emphasizing an attention to letter–sound relationships (Southgate *et al.*, 1981) that need not be the case. Instead, hearing a child read might be seen as part of a continuum developing out of shared reading but where the child now has a more prominent role as reader of the book and the teacher listens to that reading and supports and guides the child whenever it seems appropriate to do so (Campbell, 1990a).

The starting point for the development of hearing a child read, beyond a shared reading, is that the child has made advances with his/her reading so that there is not the requirement that the teacher reads the story first. There may, of course, be some discussion of the book prior to the child reading the story, but then the child reads the story to the teacher and the teacher responds to that reading by giving support and guidance whenever it is required following a miscue by the reader.

There were glimpses of the support and guidance that a teacher might provide, following miscues, in the shared reading between Richard and his teacher (there was also some confirmation of the continuum that exists between these literacy activities). First, the teacher might consider that a non-response to those miscues which retain the meaning of the text would be most appropriate. After all, the making of meaning is what the reader will be attempting to achieve.*

*The examples from the shared reading are presented in a slightly different format in order to concentrate upon the miscue of the reader and the teacher's response to that miscue, rather than including all the details from the interaction.

Richard:	In the light of the moon
	the(a) little egg lay on a leaf.
Teacher:	–

To respond to miscues such as these would be to take the reader away from his/her involvement with the story when it was not necessary to do so. However, the teacher might want to respond to those miscues which detract from the meaning of the text. But the teacher should respond in a way that creates a minimal interruption. As the reader is viewed as an active learner the teacher should support in a way that keeps the child involved with the story. One useful strategy for the teacher to use is to mediate and read part of the sentence that leads up to the miscued word, doing so with a rising intonation that invites the child back as the reader:

Richard:	one cupcake and
	one slice of salami(watermelon).
Teacher:	one slice
Richard:	one slice of watermelon.

This word cueing strategy is a simple one but it does create a minimal disruption to the reading, it informs the reader of the need to reconsider a word, but it does so by maintaining the focus upon the text. Children do appear to be helped by such teacher strategies.

At other times the teacher might simply inform the reader that the prediction had not worked, using the soft 'no' that is non-punitive but informative (Smith, 1971).

Richard:	He looked(started)
Teacher:	No.
Richard:	He starts(started)
Teacher:	Yes.
	He started

Again the use of that simple strategy worked, even though Richard just corrected the verb without also getting the verb ending correct following the teacher response.

Occasionally, too, the teacher might just provide the text word for the reader, most probably in order to maintain the flow of reading from the child.

| Richard: | out of the egg |
| | a very(came) |

Teacher:	came
Richard:	came a tiny and very hungry caterpillar.

However, the teacher would want to avoid using this particular strategy too often as it might make the reader over-reliant upon the teacher, and the purpose of the hearing-a-child-read interaction, while maintaining the interest and enjoyment of the reader, is to encourage him/her towards independent and silent reading.

Although non-response, word cueing, a soft 'no' and providing the word might predominate as the teacher's response to the reader's miscues, because they keep the child involved with the text, other strategies would also be used on occasions. And that would include calling the reader's attention to the letters and associated sounds in a word. There was a simple example of that in Richard's shared reading.

Richard:	he ate through
	two peppers(pears) //
Teacher:	They do look a bit like peppers
	And they do begin with a 'p'.
	But they might be something else, do you think?
Richard:	pineapples – eh –

In this instance the teacher responded to the reader's use of the first letter 'p' in his substitution 'peppers'(pears) by drawing attention to that letter. And Richard appeared to follow the teacher's reference to the letter 'p' with his next substitution 'pineapples'. So although the teacher's response did not help Richard on this occasion, it did serve to draw attention to the graphophonic cues. The teacher did help the learner develop a knowledge of letters and sounds.

At the end of a reading the teacher would, as with previous interactions with real books, discuss the story with the reader, make text-to-life connections and give the child the opportunity to express his/her feelings towards the story.

As each child continues to develop as a reader it will become apparent that actually listening to the child read may not be the most helpful support that the teacher can provide. Instead, the teacher and the child may just have a dialogue about the book that has been read. That will not be so different from the post-reading period indicated above. However, it will extend to comments about the structure of the story or a debate about the author and other books of a similar kind. The teacher will have in mind to encourage the future involvement of the reader with other books.

Sustained silent reading

As we have already noted, Cambourne (1988) suggested that where the first two hours of the day were devoted to language, part of that time might be given over to sustained silent reading (SSR). Since Southgate *et al.* (1981) suggested periods of personal uninterrupted reading in classrooms, there does appear to have been a developing interest in the use of SSR in the UK. For instance, Campbell (1990a) provided details from two case studies of schools where SSR in differing formats had been established and was being developed.

Teachers adopting a real books approach will want to create a time for SSR because it ensures a period when the children can engage with a book uninterrupted by other happenings in the classroom. But, of course, like other literacy activities, SSR requires a clear classroom organization. Most of the suggestions and guidelines that are offered for the organization of this activity are developments from a list provided by McCracken (1971). So what needs to be done?

First, a time needs to be set aside each day when children can engage in personal reading. Many schools are finding that a time immediately before or after a natural break in the school day is particularly appropriate (Campbell, 1990a). Then it is necessary to ensure that each child has a personally selected book at an appropriate level, and perhaps a second book available, especially for older children, if the first book is nearly completed. And that implies that there will be an adequate number of interesting books available in the classroom. The children are then made aware that they will have up to perhaps twenty-five minutes to enjoy their books uninterrupted. That time allocation may be increased gradually, although with a new class the teacher may be well advised to start with a relatively short period of SSR in order to get the children used to the activity. During the SSR time every effort is made to ensure that there is no talking or movement around the room. However, Fenwick (1988) suggested that quietness rather than silence might be the most appropriate expectation, especially for younger children. Teachers will recognize that some younger readers will read aloud even when they are reading to themselves. Nevertheless, the quietness and lack of movement do appear to be aided greatly if the teacher, and any other adults in the room, are also engaged in silent reading at the same time. Wheldall and Entwistle (1988) provided evidence from classroom studies which demonstrated the power of the teacher's acting as a silent reading role model for the children. Finally, McCracken (1971) suggested that children should be made aware that there will be no testing of the reading, that this is a time to enjoy books. Of course, the teacher and the children might want to share some of their thoughts about the story, its structure, interesting words, and so on, after the end of the silent reading, but the point is to share the enjoyment of the story, not to test.

So sustained silent reading in some format does appear to be worthwhile. But the emphasis of this book is on younger children, and questions might be raised about the effectiveness of this activity with children who may not yet be able to read in the conventional sense. Nevertheless, in such circumstances children can still enjoy the engagement with books, although many may demonstrate 'reading like behaviour' (Cambourne, 1988) rather than reading. It may also be necessary to reduce the amount of time devoted to the activity so that it commences with just two or three minutes and moves gradually to, say, ten minutes. Furthermore, Hong (1981) suggested that rather than operating with a whole class it might be more appropriate to have SSR with small groups of five to seven children when working with the youngest of school children.

However, whole classes of five- and six-year-old children have been seen operating effectively in a silent reading period. In one case their ERIC (Everyone Reading In Class) was joined by a stuffed animal, Eric, who liked to read every day. The children also wrote letters to Eric to tell him about the books that they had enjoyed reading. So reading and writing (or writing-like behaviour) connections could be made arising out of the sustained silent reading. But most importantly, the activity is used to encourage an interest and enjoyment of books.

Nursery rhymes and songs

As part of the process of shared reading with big books, Holdaway (1979) found that nursery rhymes and songs could play an important part in the activity. Initially, the use of a favourite song and a nursey rhyme or two were used to settle children into the activity. And because that worked so well one new song, poem or nursery rhyme was introduced each day during the first two weeks so that the children developed a repertoire of them. These songs and nursery rhymes were also written up as big books or sheets so that the children could see the one-to-one relationship between the written and spoken (or sung) words.

Teachers of young children will know that songs, nursery rhymes, poems and chants are useful at times other than during shared reading with big books. This use of language can not only settle children into that task but also help the teacher during the transition from one activity to another or when the children are moving off to a break or returning from one. But the use of these songs, nursery rhymes, poems, chants and language games such as 'I spy' is helpful for reasons other than purely organizational ones.

First, children enjoy the rhyming and alliteration that will be part of many of these arrangements of language. And that enjoyment will link back to earlier uses of language in games which we noted as part of childhood culture in Chapter 2. Children appear to enjoy playing with language in this way. But it may also be that during such play the children will not only be learning about rhyme, alliteration and words. They will also be developing their general awareness of language sounds, or phonological awareness (Goswami and Bryant, 1990). More particularly, the rhymes will help the children develop their ability to detect the first unit of a word (onset), and the end unit of a word (rime) – for example, 'str' and 'ing' in the word 'string'. And that developing awareness of sounds, and knowledge of letters, will enable the young reader to make use of the graphophonic cueing system when reading (as we also noted earlier in Chapter 2).

Teachers using a real books approach may not place an emphasis upon the direct teaching of phonics, but they do want to create a balance and encourage children to acquire a knowledge of letters and their associated sounds or phonemic awareness. However, they do so in the perspective of real reading, Goodman (1986) argued. And being involved with nursery rhymes and songs is part of that real reading. But children also develop their knowledge of letters and sounds and their ability to read when they are engaged in writing. This would be an appropriate moment, therefore, to turn our attention to the reading–writing connection.

CHAPTER 9

Reading–writing connections

Goodman (1986, p.47) suggested that 'reading and writing develop to-gether and support each other'. Thus the teacher with a class of young developing readers will want to ensure that as well as providing oppor-tunities for reading there is also provision for and encouragement of writ-ing. We have already noted, in Chapter 5, that a writing centre might be part of that provision and that children can be encouraged to write lists, messages, greetings cards, letters, stories or poems, produce signs and directions and write about personal events and experiences. All of that writing will be encouraged where the children can be helped to see that there is a real purpose and audience for it.

And the children can write, especially if they have the opportunity to see adults engaged in a similar process. The Baghban (1984) study of Giti learning to read and write demonstrated, as have other studies (see, for example, Bissex, 1980, Ferreiro and Teberosky, 1982, and Harste *et al.*, 1984), that children will engage in writing-type activites and, indeed, are interested in doing so. Although at first sight some of the earliest marks that are put on the page may appear to be scribbles, these 'scribbles' begin to show a difference between drawing and writing, the writing running from left to right and/or top to bottom and with letters beginning to become more apparent.

Those letters begin to become part of the child's invented spellings and form part of the the earliest written communcations from the child. 'RUDF' (Are you deaf?) from five-year-old Paul to his mother is one of the better-known examples (Bissex, 1980). But Robert's 'I. h. s. e. w.' (I have seen a witch) which he produced in the classroom, also at five years of age, demonstrates how children use their growing knowledge of letters and sounds to construct writing (Robinson, 1989). Furthermore, this use of invented spelling in the classroom means that the child has to pay very close attention to individual letters and their associated sounds, so that phonemic awareness is encouraged. In addition, when the child is reading from a real book, although the main cues might be extracted from the semantic and syntactic ones, the graphophonic cues will tend to be used more frequently.

A teacher using a real books approach will want to make connections between the stories read in the classroom and the children's writing. To illustrate the making of this connection we can explore some children's writing derived from their enjoyment of *Rosie's Walk*. (These examples are taken from an infants' class with thirty-two children, aged five and six, at the start of their second year of schooling in England). This is a well-loved story which young children never seem to tire of hearing. And yet, as Graham (1991) indicated, the pictures tell as much of the story as do the thirty-two words of the story all in one sentence, for although there are two main characters only one, Rosie the hen, is mentioned in the writing. The fox, who is very important to the story, only appears in the illustrations.

The story reads:

Rosie the hen went for a walk
across the yard
around the pond
over the haycock
past the mill
through the fence
under the beehives
and got back in time for dinner.

With each reading young children seem to get something more from the story. They display their excitement in the adventures of the hen and the misadventures of the fox, their humour as they enjoy some of the episodes and their pleasure in the outcome of the story.

The teacher can encourage the children's involvement with the story by providing the opportunity for the children to tell about the story, to rewrite the story in their own words and/or to express their feelings about the tale. Not only will the writing differ from each child who writes about the story therefore, but the amount of support from the teacher will also vary quite considerably.

Some children, when they become more sophisticated in their understanding of letters and words, appear to be less willing to engage in invented spelling and instead seek out the teacher as a scribe. Sarah did just that when she used the teacher as a scribe and model for her own writing. Nevertheless, Sarah was able to tell about the plot and to provide an episode from that plot, albeit that her writing was constrained by the overuse of the connective 'and':

One day Rosie went for
a walk and a fox
was going to chase
her and she went
over the haystack and
the fox fell in.

In contrast to the writing from Sarah, John wrote more confidently on his own about the story and of his feelings towards it. His writing, without a model, is in the original more difficult to decipher. Nevertheless, he demonstrated his growing knowledge of language by the inclusion of a number of words which were not part of the story but might be implied from the illustrations, such as 'decided', 'sneaked', and 'stalking'. He also used the connectives 'but' and 'because' as well as 'and'.

One day Rosie decided to go for
a walk but the fox sneaked up
on Rosie but the fox was
still stalking and a bag of
flour fell on top of him.

I like the story
because a bag of
flour fell on him.

Other children in the class also produced some writing about the story at various levels and with greater or lesser support from the teacher. An important feature of the classroom organization for the children's writing was that the children were aware that there would be a real purpose and audience for their writing. The children knew that their writing would be placed in one or more books so that other children would be able to read their contribution. Furthermore, they were aware that the teacher would also extract some of the words that they had written to create a running story for the complete book.

As an example of that procedure, Sarah's writing eventually formed the first page, of a class book called 'Rosie's Walk'. Alongside Sarah's writing and underneath the picture she had drawn the teacher had written in thick felt pen:

One day Rosie
went for a walk.

Thus Sarah's first seven words had also formed the basis for the start of the class book. Each child could see very clearly that his/her writing was valued. Furthermore, the actual words that they had written could be seen to contribute very directly to the development of a class book which was then available for them and for others to read. The class book to which Sarah had contributed read:

> *One day Rosie*
> *went for a walk*
> *Rosie walked over*
> *the haystack but*
> *the fox fell in it.*
> *Rosie went past*
> *the pond.*
> *The fox fell in*
> *the pond and Rosie*
> *walked on.*
> *Rosie walked across*
> *the fields and the*
> *fox chased her.*
> *A bag of flour fell*
> *on top of the fox.*

Of course, the children's rewriting did not have the same rhythm and quality as the original book. But it was constructed from their own words. And, as Burman (1990a) argued, such class book-making has many very positive benefits, which include the development of a 'sense of ownership' and the encouragement of an understanding about books, how they are made and what it means to be an author and illustrator. Furthermore, once this book was bound it could be added to others that had been written collaboratively by the children. Those texts, well known by the children, formed part of the class library corner for their own and visitors' use.

The teacher and the children need not stop reflecting upon the stories they have read or listened to once they have written about them. After all, if Rosie can go for a walk then so, too, can the children with their teacher. The link to the story that the children had enjoyed is obvious and it provides the basis for further writing. So text-to-life and life-to-text experieces were developed, which enabled the children to extend their understanding of and ability with literacy.

After the walk Michael wrote on his own about some of the animals and objects that he had seen:

> *We went for a walk and we saw*
> *rabbit hopping in the grass*
> *to look for carrots.*
> *We went past the*
> *church in the yard*
> *we saw graves.*

An important feature of that writing was Michael's use of his observations and the word 'graves'. The use of an organic vocabulary (Ashton-Warner, 1963) with its deep and powerful meanings can be a product of engaging children in a variety of experiences from which they are encouraged to write. And, as we have seen, some of that vocabulary will demonstrate the children's intrinsic interests and may be far removed from the vocabulary typically found in school books for five- and six-year-old children.

The children's walk with their teacher provided them with a stimulus for writing as well as for drawing, painting and play activities. As with their involvement with *Rosie's Walk*, and their subsequent writing on that occasion, the children knew that their writing was not just a product for the teacher to read but would form the basis for one or more class books. Again the same principles were adopted; each child's writing and art work was valued and was stuck into a book. The teacher used some of the words from each child in order to construct a class book for the other children to read, and the books were made available in the class library.

One of the class books from the classroom on this occasion was called 'We went for a walk':

> *We walked*
> *through the*
> *lane.*
> *We saw the*
> *trees fallen*
> *down.*
> *We walked past*
> *the busy road.*
> *We went past*
> *the church.*
> *We walked*
> *across the road*
> *and saw a horse.*
> *We went down*
> *the road and*
> *past the shops*
> *and back to school.*

It is interesting to note how the last four lines of this class book to an extent followed some of the rhythm of *Rosie's Walk*. An involvement with stories can encourage the children to reflect upon and use some of the rhythms and language of other authors. And the teacher did not shy away from some of the more powerful concepts that the children had written about. A number of class books were produced, one of which, entitled 'Our Walk', ended rather more sombrely with the sentence:

*We saw the
graveyard.*

But the making of books in the classroom does not always have to be a class activity. Individual book-making can also be used to encourage literacy development (Burman, 1990a). Where each child is given the opportunity to write about something which is of particular interest to him/her then there can be a real motivation to write. Here, too, the child will have an awareness of a genuine audience in that the book can become part of the class library. And being aware of an audience and making decisions about the text as it is written means that the children will be working as authors. That role as an author serves as a very sound basis, for each child, for further growth in literacy development (Hall, 1989).

In the example that we have explored in some detail it was a story that provided the starting point for the children's writing. And many of the children produced writing in a narrative format as a first response to the story. However, following their own walk some of the children moved into descriptive or report writing and it is important that children experience writing which makes different demands upon them. Hall (1989) argued that children spend far more time writing stories than they do other text, yet writing in other genres can make interesting intellectual demands upon them. Furthermore Donaldson (1989) extended that view to suggest that children who write only in narrative or descriptive forms are being deprived. Impersonal writing with the language of systematic thought is an important attribute to develop.

But are we now moving away from the early development of literacy? Probably not, for the teacher adopting a real books approach may use real books as a starting point but would be aware of the need to encourage a wide range of writing (as we noted at the beginning of this chapter) in order to support reading and encourage the fullest possible development of literacy. Such writing would include lists, messages, greetings cards and letters, and would move on to reports based on observations of objects, events and happenings. Such writing would, in part, be linked to the interests and experiences of the children and to themes being developed within the classroom. Such language experience approaches form the basis for the next chapter.

CHAPTER 10

Language experience approaches

In Chapter 9 it was shown how the real books or stories that were available in the classsroom might be used as a basis for making reading and writing connections. The stories can and do provide the foundation for developing children's literacy and they do so by capturing the interest and attention of the child. However, the story can be used also to serve as a springboard for other activities and experiences, so in the simple example we looked at the teacher took the children for a walk, just like Rosie. And that experience, and the observations that were made by the children, provided the basis for writing and for further reading. Of course, the link to *Rosie's Walk* could have been extended and a visit to a farm to see the hens, and other animals, might have opened up a wide range of other writing and reading possibilities. It might also have suggested other stories that might be read to the children, to build on that shared experience.

So from a single story, experienced by all the children in the class, a whole range of literacy activities can be generated. But, of course, each child brings to the classroom many other different interests and experiences derived from a variety of sources. And the teacher will want to utilize many of these interests and experiences, as well as providing other experiences in the classroom and outside on visits, in order to encourage the development of literacy.

A number of different approaches, such as the language experience approach, Breakthrough to Literacy and thematic work, have been used in classrooms in order to encourage literacy. But the common thread of such approaches is to work with the experiences of the child and to provide a classroom organization that allows the child to explore further those experiences through reading and writing. They are approaches that link naturally to reading real books and many teachers using story books may utilize some aspect of these approaches at the same time.

Language experience approach

In her book, on the language experience approach, Goddard (1974) emphasized the need to make use of children's feelings, interests and experiences as a fundamental part of developing their literacy. Such an approach links together speaking, listening, reading and writing and therefore helps children see the connections between those modalities of language.

Stated in its simplest form, the language experience approach is based on the notions that what the child has experienced and thought about, or the interests that have been developed, can be talked about; that what is talked about can be expressed in other ways, whether through drawing, painting or writing; that what the child writes (or has written for him/her) can be read by the child and perhaps by other children.

As an example, Goddard gives an account of a class of children who arrived at school excited by the very strong wind that they had experienced that morning. One child, with support from the teacher, wrote:

> On a windy day the trees bend and the leaves fall off the trees and when the wind blows I go cold, I cover my face up and run home and get near the fire and lie down by the fire and when I lie in bed the wind goes Shoo, I can hear it. (p128)

Such an example suggests that the experiences of the children can be used to good effect to encourage writing and subsequently reading. It was the links between written language as talk written down and the production of writing for reading in a natural way which led Holdaway (1979) to write about the language experience approach in a positive manner. However, he did also recognize some of the problems associated with the approach. In particular, he suggested that the endless stories about such things as going to the shops or visiting the fire station make for dull reading and writing.

For instance, the child who tells the teacher about a shopping expedition may well be relating a real and interesting event in which they had participated:

> I went to the shops with my mummy.

However, if that becomes the regular contribution from the child then the literacy opportunities for the child have become as stilted and limiting as might be provided by the most pedestrian of reading schemes. And it is for such reasons that Goddard (1974) suggested that, although the teacher might start with the interests and experiences that the children bring to the school, it is part of the teacher's role to stimulate and extend the children's interests. So taking advantage of local events and major happenings beyond the locality of the school, going on visits and bringing animals, objects, materials and experiments into the classroom will all be utilized to extend the children's interests and experiences and provide the basis for worthwhile literacy activities.

Nevertheless, a further problem exists if the teacher attempts to write down for the children their dictated commentary. In the first instance the problem is the practical one created by the difficulty of acting as scribe for all the children in the class when there may be thirty children (or more) in that class. Then there is the need to make the writing purposeful. The children need to recognize that their writing will be used for others to read, as part of a class newspaper, as part of a book, or as part of some diplay. However, there is, in addition, the question of whether it is in the best interests of the children for the teacher to act as a scribe. Yetta Goodman (1991) suggested that with our new knowledge about the composing process in writing and children's use of invented spellings it might be better for the children to do more of their own scribing. Such involvement with the process of writing does encourage the children to think about letters, words and sentences. It thus helps them on the road towards independence in writing and reading.

Nevertheless, although there may be some concerns about the language experience approach becoming ritualized, without purpose, and therefore less effective, the principles of the idea suggest that teachers following a real books approach would want to use this as part of the classroom activities. Using the children's interests and experiences, extending those interests and experiences both inside and outside of the classroom, getting the children to talk about and then write about those experiences, and using their writings whenever possible as reading material for them and for others are all worthwhile.

In some classrooms teachers have utilized what is often regarded as a commercial variation of the language experience approach. We will therefore consider Breakthrough to Literacy briefly in the next section.

Breakthrough to Literacy

Breakthrough, the shortened title commonly used by teachers in school, was introduced at the beginning of the 1970s (Mackay, Thompson and Schaub, 1970). As a practical material in the classroom, it allowed children to construct sentences using the sentence maker and printed single words and therefore to develop personal and meaningful written language from a very early stage in their schooling. These materials, and the blank cards for the teacher to provide particular words for individuals, enabled children to overcome what might have been seen as the major early impediments to writing, namely handwriting and spelling.

However, for the reasons cited above (Goodman, 1991) it might now seem more appropriate for young children to be engaged in the actual processs of writing and actively considering sentences and words as well as letters and sounds, in order to produce invented spellings, rather than manipulating pieces of card.

So why mention Breakthrough to Literacy at all in this book? First, because it was derived from the tradition of language experience approaches and it might, therefore, be seen as a logical development of language experience. And second, because one of the recognized exponents of the real books approach (Waterland, 1988) utilized it as part of the literacy provision in her classroom alongside the apprenticeship shared readings.

The attractions of Breakthrough are obvious. It does enable young children to produce written language relatively easily, and it encourages them to think about language structures. As Donaldson (1989) suggested, children's awareness of language is raised as they are helped to notice such features as word boundaries, word order, bound morphemes (-s, -ed, -ing, etc.), and all while producing meaningful writing. Furthermore, that understanding about writing occurs without the child being reliant upon the teacher-as-scribe (Waterland, 1988). It would appear to be this independence from the teacher and the opportunity for children to play with print that leads Waterland to argue for its use.

However, the Bullock Report (DES, 1975), while recognizing the value of Breakthrough as a starting point for some teachers, questioned whether the teacher would need this particular material once a language experience approach had been established in the classroom. And as has been indicated above, the child acting as his/her own scribe and therefore actively constructing written language is encouraged to forge an independence from the teacher and to think about language structures. The many examples of young children's early writing (see, for example, Hall, 1989) give evidence of the value of encouraging children to write about their feelings, interests and experiences from the earliest moment.

Some of that writing might be centred upon a theme. And thematic work will be a feature of the real books approach. It will be so because it starts with the language and knowledge of the children and builds upon that base.

Thematic work

The benefit of engaging in a topic or theme for a period of time is that it gives a 'depth of experience and time for reflection – out of which all good written expression arises' (Holdaway, 1979, p.145). Staying with a theme allows the child to be involved with an experience and to consider the vocabulary and concepts of that theme and to discuss it with others. That involvement provides a good basis for both written and artistic expression.

The thematic work will be derived from a number of different sources. A story read to the class can provide the starting point for a theme to be developed within the classroom. But the interest of an individual child or the stimulus which a teacher provides and which is developed then with the whole class might also be the starting point.

Holdaway (1979) indicated the way in which a story might develop into a theme. *The Very Hungry Caterpillar* captured the interest of a class and that interest was maintained by having the real experience of a caterpillar pupating in the classroom. That then acted as a stimulus to have other insects in the classroom and to observe and discuss their life cycles.

In another classroom *The Very Hungry Caterpillar* has been seen by the author to be used as the basis for a theme. The five-year-old children produced a very large frieze with caterpillars and butterflies on one wall of the classroom. They produced a book of caterpillar stories, like this one:

> Once upon a time a caterpillar was sleeping in the sun then he looked for food. (Adrian)

But they also produced writing that was in a more scientific mode, such as:

> In the pupa the caterpillar is changing. (Michelle)

This writing formed the basis for a book called 'The story of a butterfly.'

In addition, the children made models of caterpillars and then measured them using a variety of standards of measurement:

> My caterpillar is 3 of my feet long. (Victoria)

So in this example the five-year-old children were able to listen, talk, read, and write about caterpillars at their level of understanding. They were also able to engage in art, craft, science and mathematics in some form. So the story provided a good basis for a real involvement with a theme.

Where the theme originates from an individual child and is pursued solely by that child then, at least initially, the child may need some assistance in planning for the theme. Burman (1990a) suggested that the teacher working alongside the child might produce a web (or flow chart) in order to help organize the child's thinking. It would also serve to provide a plan for the sequence of the child's book. As an example Burman (1990a, p.51) provided the web produced by Claire with her teacher:

What Claire knows a lot about.

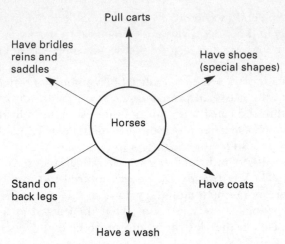

Claire was then able to produce a book written and illustrated directly from her own interests and experience, but, importantly, sustained over a period of time so that the depth of experience and the opportunity for reflection extended the theme well beyond the 'I went shopping with my mummy' contribution.

In order to emphasize the collaborative nature of learning the teacher will occasionally develop a class theme, although the impetus for that theme may come from various sources. An event external to the school, the stimulus provided by the teacher or the enthusiasms of the children are all possibilities as starting points. Goddard (1974) provided an example where the impetus came from the children. The class had a movement and music lesson on pirates and the sea. That created an interest in making a pirate boat. And from that start a whole range of activities followed: collecting pictures of galleons of the sixteenth century; making a treasure chest, collecting, sorting, counting and measuring items as the treasure; making hats and cutlasses; painting a large sea frieze; making up a story 'This is a pirate island'; making a book of pirate stories and pictures; and making a papier mâché island. So a wide range of reading, writing, mathematics, stories and dramatic play was developed from the interest of the class in pirates.

What is evident is that using the interests and experiences of the children in a language experience or thematic approach does provide a good deal of opportunity for speaking, listening, reading and writing to some purpose. It therefore provides the basis for the development of literacy. But the teacher will want to keep some record of the progress in literacy that is being made by each of the children in the class. Assessment forms the basis of the next chapter.

CHAPTER 11

Assessment

The teacher in the real books classroom will, like any other teacher, want to make an assessment of the progress that is being made by each child in reading and writing. That assessment will be of immediate importance for at least two reasons. First, the teacher will be assessing the reading and writing of each child because he/she will wish to support, guide and facilitate that reading and writing as it occurs. The very nature of teaching requires the teacher to know what the child is attempting and to decide on the best response to those efforts. But beyond that, and second, the teacher will want to build up a knowledge of what the child appears to be achieving so that future experiences and teaching in the classroom can match the child's apparent needs. As a result of making these assessments the teacher will, of course, be well placed to report on the progress of the child to parents, teachers and others who may have a right to know about the literacy progress within the classroom.

But how will this assessment of progress take place on a day-to-day basis? The teacher will observe, interact and analyse (Goodman, 1989) both on an informal and a formal basis. As a result, the teacher will record and evaluate the progress of each child but also gain insights into the effectiveness of the classroom activities.

The teacher will be making informal observations throughout the school day, both from a distance and also from a more intimate perspective. After all, knowing about the children and managing the classroom activities will be dependent upon such informal observations. From a distance the teacher will note that Sally, Susan and Tony are reading quietly in the library corner but that Michael hasn't yet settled on an activity. If that lack of involvement on Michael's part were to persist then, of course, the teacher would want to encourage Michael towards some learning activity and particularly towards literacy events. Closer at hand, the teacher might note the children's efforts as they write. One child might be seen to be holding a pencil rather awkwardly, another beginning to use a dictionary as a support for writing: in each instance the teacher might mediate briefly to give some support and guidance.

More formally, the teacher might decide to note, on a list, the children who use the library corner during the course of a day. Who does not spend some time reading? How can they be encouraged to read on their own? The observations that are made by teachers help them develop a picture of some of the progress that is being made by the children in literacy.

Informal interactions will often be a product of the observations that are made by the teacher. So the teacher might join a group of writers for a moment to assist where necessary or to ask some 'what if . . . ?' questions, which help the children think beyond their present writing. At times, of course, an informal interaction will be initiated by a child who seeks the guidance of the teacher about a word, a sentence or an idea. But, it is, perhaps, the formal planned interactions which are the vitally important ones for encouraging the children's literacy development and for inform-ing the teacher about the children's progress.

A story reading, for instance, will tell about the children who concen-trate on and appear to enjoy a story and/or who comment upon the pictures or story. Shared readings will give the teacher detailed information on the children's emerging reading. A knowledge of left-to-right orienta-tion, using the pictures or story to predict events, recognition of words and sentences, use of initial letters to predict a word, developments towards more conventional readings, ability to retell a story, and so on, will all be made evident during the course of a shared reading. And teachers who have informed themselves about miscue analysis will find that they have become more sensitive to the miscues that are produced by children and can evaluate those miscues as the reading proceeds. Discussions about what has been read, or what has been written, will also add to the teacher's knowledge of the child as a literacy user.

So the beginnings of an informal analyses of the children's reading may occur during a shared reading just as an informal analysis might occur as the teacher sees a child writing who, using his/her knowledge of letters and sounds, spells words in particular ways. The knowledge of teachers about the general stages of spelling development (see, for example, Graves, 1983) will help in that analysis. But the teacher will also want to engage in a more formal analysis of progress from time to time.

Therefore, the teacher will occasionally use a shared reading not nec-essarily to support the reader but to take a running record of the reading (Clay, 1985) or to tape-record the reading without support and then ana-lyse the miscues (see, for example, Goodman *et al.*, 1987). In particular, that analysis will give the teacher insights into the use that the child is making of the semantic, syntactic and graphophonic cue systems.

The teacher will sometimes also want to analyse the children's writing in a more systematic way. Maintaining a writing portfolio for each child in the class, and, indeed, throughout the child's years in the school, is a useful way of detecting progress and determining needs. A sample of writing from each child might be collected every term or month and then analysed for organization of ideas, awareness of audience, spelling, use of language conventions such as punctuation, use of cohesive devices, and, for stories, the use of an appropriate story structure (Wilkinson *et al.* (1980) have provided a detailed model for the analysis of writing). Importantly, the teacher would need to note the context in which the writing for the portfolio took place. In particular, the amount of support that the child received from the teacher, other adults and/or children needs to be noted.

The London *Primary Language Record* (CLPE, 1988) provides a very comprehensive means of recording the language progress of children in talking, listening, reading and writing. Staff in primary schools might well consider whether the use of that framework would best serve the needs of the children. However, if somewhat less detail were required then miscue analysis and writing portfolios would provide a basis for the records that the teacher might keep in the classroom. Additionally, a more regular record of the shared readings might also be maintained so that the teacher has a note of the books read and the developing strategies of the reader. Thus for our earlier example of Richard sharing *The Very Hungry Caterpillar*, the teacher might record that reading on to a reading card which would be used to provide a picture of Richard's reading throughout the school year, recording as it would each shared reading with the teacher:

Richard

Date	Book	Comments
9 Oct	*The Very Hungry Caterpillar.*	Moving to a more conventional reading. Evidence of all three cue systems being used. Peppers-pineapples(pears). A grocery shop in the home corner might be useful.

Even as a single entry the record is of some value and points to other literacy activities as well as recording details of the reading. However, it is when a collection of entries is made over time that the record then becomes most valuable in showing the developments and needs of the child.

Had the teacher kept a running record of Richard's reading of *The Very Hungry Caterpillar* then that would have given a more detailed picture of his reading. Furthermore, it would then have allowed for a more precise miscue analysis to have been made. The running record might begin as follows:

In the light of the moon	T / T / / / *
a little egg lay on a leaf.	the-the T / / / / /
One Sunday morning the warm	/ Summer's day / /
sun came up and pop out of the egg	/ / out / / T / / /
came a tiny and very hungry caterpillar.	a very(T) / / / / / /
He started to look for some food.	/ looked-starts / / /O/
On Monday	/ /
he ate through	/ / /
one apple.	/ /
But he was still	/ / / /
hungry.	/
On Tuesday	/ /
he ate through	/ /
two pears,	/ peppers-
	-pineapples(T)
but he was	/ / /
still hungry.	/ /

Conventions:

/	word read correctly
T	word told by the teacher
the	substituted word
looked-starts	substitution sequence
O	omission of word
SC	would be used to indicate a self-correction

The running record would confirm the view of the teacher that Richard was moving towards a conventional reading of the text and that he was using all three cue systems. Each of the substitutions that Richard produced maintained the sentence structure and meaning of the book. Furthermore, there was evidence of his growing phonemic awareness, with the substitutions of Summer's(Sunday) and peppers–pineapples(pears). Of course, the teacher was more involved with this reading than might be the case where a detailed miscue analysis was being conducted. Nevertheless, it does demonstrate the way in which more information can be collected on the child's reading development, at intervals, by using a more formal interaction and analysis.

Similarly, the writing samples would help the teacher determine the child's writing development at that point and over time. Two examples from five-year-old Michael demonstrate the value of keeping a writing portfolio:

Michael 6 Oct	Working in a small group with each child telling his/her story to the group and then working independently on the writing.

Once upon a time
There was 3 pigs
and They saw
The fox
he blew The house
down

Michael 24 Nov	Independent writing of a story, initiated by Michael.

Once There was a robber he got in
To The house To geT The money
From The house and The man
phoned The police and The police
caughT The robber in The
house and Took him To prison

Those two pieces of writing, produced some seven weeks apart, demonstrate a growth in Michael's writing. There was a greater development of the story plot and setting, with a logical and extended sequencing of events in the second story. It is not possible to say whether Michael had sorted out the use of was/were, but his letter formation and spacing had developed during the seven weeks. The teacher, while wishing to maintain and encourage the flow of writing, would also have in mind to help Michael with his use of upper- and lower-case letters, especially the letter 't'/'T'; to develop a firmer understanding of sentences and the punctuation used to denote such (this might be achieved through discussion after shared readings); and to use cohesive ties other than 'and' (which might be encouraged by particular forms of writing, particularly reporting). Subsequent samples of written work would demonstrate whether those needs had been met.

The analyses are conducted, as we have noted above, in order that the teacher can make an evaluation of the progress in reading and writing that each child is making. And collectively those results will indicate to the teacher whether any aspects of the literacy curriculum are being missed by the current organization and management of the classroom. These evaluations will enable the teacher to plan further for literacy activities in the classroom.

CHAPTER 12

The importance of the teacher

As we noted in the introduction to this book, a real books approach has been mistakenly regarded as a non-teaching approach to the development of children's literacy. Such a view could not be further from the truth.

It will have become very evident, during the course of this book, that the teacher's role is very demanding and diverse when a real books approach is adopted. The teacher does not just stand back and let the learning take place. Instead he/she is involved in a substantial number of decisions about the activities within the classroom. Let us briefly remind ourselves of some of these roles.

The teacher has to know about books for he/she will want to be involved in the selection of the books for the classroom. And as we noted, not all scheme books should be rejected nor all non-scheme books accepted. The language, the storyline and illustrations all need to be considered. Then the teacher will need to know about children and, in particular, how they develop as readers. This is important because, once engaged upon shared readings, the teacher will need to determine the structure of the shared reading, to decide upon the nature of the discussions, to analyse the miscues produced by the reader and to consider the best ways to respond to those miscues for that child at that point in his/her development. Throughout the shared reading the teacher will have been encouraging, supporting, guiding and facilitating the learning of the young reader.

The teacher will also have established and maintained links with the parents and have developed an appropriate line of communication with them. All of that will require careful planning and organization, and these skills will need to be very evident also in the classroom. Organizing the literacy areas and activities in the classroom are of prime importance and the subsequent management of those is needed to ensure that they can be put to best use.

Preparing and developing the environmental and classroom print, together with the materials for the literacy play activities, is very time-consuming. Furthermore, it requires the teacher's attention throughout the school year in order to ensure that interest is maintained in the various forms of print.

Selecting a book and planning a time for story reading are important prerequisites. But during the reading the teacher will need to put on a first class performance as intonation and pitch, speed of delivery, responses to comments and questions, and the showing of the pictures are all used to involve the children in the story. The same teaching skills will be important when the teacher engages the children in other classroom interactions centred on literacy.

The various opportunities that are provided for writing, whether linked to a story book or based on language experience approaches and/or thematic work, do not just happen. They require planning, preparation and managing. Furthermore, during the writing, just as during sessions of reading, the teacher will be observing, interacting, analysing and recording. And that is done so that the teacher will be able to evaluate the progress of each child and, collectively, the effectiveness of the classroom activities.

A real books approach is not an easy option for a teacher. It may be rewarding and enjoyable for the teacher and the children but for the teacher it is also demanding. It requires subtle and sophisticated teaching.

Postscript

This book has concentrated upon the development of reading in young children while using a real books approach to learning. It has been argued that a real books approach does not just consist of the books to be read and shared readings. There are a range of organizational features and literacy activities which are recognized to be part of the approach but which sometimes seem to be omitted in any discussion on the subject. Those features and activities were debated in this book.

A real books approach is one that argues for the centrality of language and literacy in the early years curriculum. It should not be surprising, therefore, that teachers who utilize real books would want to organize and manage the classroom in a way which emphasizes language and literacy. Development in those areas provides the foundation for most of the subsequent learning.

During the writing of this book two relevant reports were published. First, the National Curriculum Council (NCC, 1991, p.5) indicated that 'A reduction in the time for teaching reading was frequently noted as being a result of introducing new areas into the primary curriculum'. That was a major concern: reading must remain a priority. Then, the Education, Science and Arts Committee of the House of Commons (ESAC, 1991, p.viii) concluded 'that the claim that reading standards [in England and Wales] have fallen in recent years has not been proved beyond reasonable doubt'. That was good news but insufficient, because all teachers of young children have as a prime aim the development of reading. And teachers using real books will want, like all other teachers, to raise reading standards and to encourage children to keep reading once they are independent readers. It is an aspiration that is shared by the author of this book.

References

Amery, H, and Cartwright, S. (1989) *The Naughty Sheep*. London: Usborne Publishing.

Arnold, H. (1982) *Listening to Children Reading*. Sevenoaks: Hodder and Stoughton.

Ashton-Warner, S. (1963) *Teacher*. London: Secker and Warburg.

Baghban, M. (1984) *Our Daughter Learns to Read and Write*. Newark, Delaware: International Reading Association.

Bissex, G. (1980) *Gnys at Wrk: A Child Learns to Read and Write*. Cambridge, Mass.: Harvard University Press.

Bloom, W. (1987) *Partnership with Parents in Reading*. Sevenoaks: Hodder and Stoughton.

Bruner, J. S. (1986) *Actual Minds, Possible Worlds*. Cambridge, Mass.: Harvard University Press.

Burman, C. (1990a) Organizing for reading 3–7. In B. Wade (ed.) *Reading for Real*. Milton Keynes: Open University Press.

Burman, C. (1990b) Support for real reading. In B. Wade (ed.) *Reading for Real*. Milton Keynes: Open University Press.

Cambourne, B. (1988) *The Whole Story: Natural Learning and the Acquisition of Literacy in the Classroom*. Auckland: Ashton Scholastic.

Campbell, R. (1987) Oral reading errors of two young beginning readers, *Journal of Research in Reading*, 10 (2).

Campbell, R. (1988) *Hearing Children Read*. London: Routledge.

Campbell, R. (1990a) *Reading Together*. Milton Keynes: Open University Press.

Campbell, R. (1990b) *Phonics, Standards and Real Books*. An occasional paper of the Exmouth Seminar. Polytechnic South West.

Carle, E. (1969) *The Very Hungry Caterpillar*. New York: Philomel Books.

Cashdan, A. (1990) The great unproven failure, *Education*, 28 September.

Chall, J. S. (1967) *Learning to Read: The Great Debate*. New York: McGraw-Hill.

Clark, M. M. (1976) *Young Fluent Readers*. London: Heinemann Educational.

Clay, M. M. (1972) *Reading: The Patterning of Complex Behaviour*. London: Heinemann Educational.

Clay, M. M. (1985) *The Early Detection of Reading Difficulties*. Auckland: Heinemann Educational.

CLPE (1988) *The Primary Language Record*. London: Centre for Language in Primary Education.

Coles, M. (1990) The 'real books' approach: is apprenticeship a weak analogy? *Reading*, 24 (2).

Cowland, J. (1991) How innovations are interpreted, *Reading*, 25 (1).

Cox, B. (1990) Misread evidence, *Times Educational Supplement*, 28 September.

Davis, C. and Stubbs, R. (1988) *Shared Reading in Practice*. Milton Keynes: Open University Press.

DES (1967) *Children and their Primary Schools* (Plowden Report). London: HMSO.

DES (1975) *A Language for Life* (Bullock Report). London: HMSO.

DES (1990) *English in the National Curriculum*. London: HMSO.

Dombey, H. (1987) Reading for real from the start, *English in Education*, 21 (2).

Dombey, H. (1988) Partners in the telling. In M. Meek and C. Mills (eds) *Language and Literacy in the Primary School*. Lewes: The Falmer Press.

Dombey, H. (1990) Up the garden path, *Times Educational Supplement*, 23 November.

Donaldson, M. (1978) *Children's Minds*. London: Fontana.

Donaldson, M. (1989) *Sense and Sensibility*. Reading: Reading and Language Information Centre, University of Reading School of Education.

ESAC (1991) *Standards of Reading in Primary Schools*. Third Report of the House of Commons Education, Science and Arts Committee. London: HMSO.

Fenwick, G. (1988) *Uninterrupted Sustained Silent Reading*. Reading: Reading and Language Information Centre.

Ferreiro, E. (1990) Literacy Development: Psychogenesis. In Y. Goodman (ed.) *How Children Construct Literacy*. Newark, Delaware: International Reading Association.

Ferreiro, E. and Teberosky, A. (1982) *Literacy Before Schooling*. London: Heinemann.

Fox, C. (1988) Poppies will make them Grant. In M. Meek. and C. Mills (eds) *Language and Literacy in the Primary School*. Lewes: Falmer Press.

Goddard, N. (1974) *Literacy: Language-Experience Approaches*. London: Macmillan Educational.

Gollasch, F. V. (1982) *Language and Literacy. The Selected Writings of Kenneth S. Goodman*, Vols 1 and 2. London: Routledge and Kegan Paul.

Goodman, K. (1967) Reading: a psycholinguistic guessing game, *The Journal of the Reading Specialist*, 6 (4).

Goodman, K. (1986) *What's Whole in Whole Language?* Portsmouth, New Hampshire: Heinemann Educational.

Goodman, K., Goodman, Y. and Hood, W. (1989) *The Whole Language Evaluation Book*. Portsmouth, New Hampshire: Heinemann Educational.

Goodman, Y., Watson, D. and Burke, C. (1987) *Reading Miscue Inventory: Alternative Procedures*. New York: Richard Owen.

Goodman, Y. (1989) Evaluation of students. In K. Goodman, Y. Goodman, and W. Hood (eds) *The Whole Language Evaluation Book*. Portsmouth, New Hampshire: Heinemann Educational.

Goodman, Y. (1991) The History of Whole Language. In K. Goodman, L. Bridges Bird and Y. Goodman (eds) *The Whole Language Catalog*. Santa Rosa, Calif.: American School Publishers.

Goswami, U. C. and Bryant, P. (1990) *Phonological Skills and Learning to Read*. Hove: Lawrence Erlbaum Associates.

Graham, J. (1991) *Pictures on the Page*. Sheffield: NATE Publications.

Graves, D. H. (1983) *Writing: Teachers and Children at Work*. Portsmouth, New Hampshire: Heinemann Educational.

Hall, N. (1987) *The Emergence of Literacy*. Sevenoaks: Hodder and Stoughton.

Hall, N. (1989) *Writing with Reason: The Emergence of Authorship in Young Children*. London: Hodder and Stoughton.

Harris, A. J. (1979) The effective teacher of reading, revisited, *The Reading Teacher*, 33 (2).

Harrison, C. (1991) The state of reading – a personal view, *Language and Literacy News*, (4).

Harste, J. C, Woodward, V. A. and Burke, C. L. (1984) *Language Stories and Literacy Lessons*. Portsmouth, New Hampshire: Heinemann Educational.

Heath, M. (1985) Communication between home and school, *Reading*, 19 (2).

Hewison, J. and Tizard, S. (1980) Parental involvement and reading attainment, *British Journal of Educational Psychology*, 50.

HMI (1990) *The Teaching and Learning of Reading in Primary Schools*. London: DES.

Holdaway, D. (1979) *The Foundations of Literacy*. London: Ashton Scholastic.

Hong, L. R. (1981) Modifying SSR for beginning readers, *The Reading Teacher*, 34 (8).

Hudson, J. (1988) Real books for real readers for real purposes, *Reading*, 22 (2).

Hutchins, P. (1969) *Rosie's Walk*. London: Bodley Head.

Hutchins, P. (1973) *Goodnight Owl*. London: Bodley Head.

Jackson, A. and Hannon, P. W. (1981) *The Bellfield Reading Project*. Rochdale: Bellfield Community Council.

Laminack, L. L. (1991) *Learning with Zachary*. Richmond Hill, Ontario: Scholastic.

McCracken, R. A. (1971) Initiating sustained silent reading, *Journal of Reading Behaviour*, 14.

Mackay, D., Thomson, B. and Schaub, P. (1970) *Breakthrough to Literacy*. London: Schools Council/Longman.

M'Culloch, J. M. (1852) *First Reading Book*. Edinburgh: Oliver and Boyd.

Martin, T. (1989) *The Strugglers*. Milton Keynes: Open University Press.

Mason, J. M., Peterman, C. L. and Kerr, B. M. (1989) Reading to kindergarten children. In D. S. Strickland and L. M. Morrow (eds) *Emerging Literacy: Young Children Learn to Read and Write*. Newark, Delaware: International Reading Association.

Meek, M. (1982) *Learning to Read*. London: Bodley Head.

Meek, M. (1984) Forward. In J. Trelease (ed.) *The Read Aloud Handbook*. Harmondsworth: Penguin.

Meek, M. (1988) *How Texts Teach What Readers Learn*. Stroud: Thimble Press.

Money, T. (1988) Early literacy. In G. M. Blenkin and A. V. Kelly (eds) *Early Childhood Education: A Developmental Curriculum*. London: Paul Chapman.

Morrow, L. M. (1989) Designing the classroom to promote literacy development. In D. S. Strickland and L. M. Morrow (eds) *Emerging Literacy: Young Children Learn to Read and Write*. Newark, Delaware: International Reading Association.

Morrow, L. M. and Rand M. K. (1991) Promoting literacy during play by designing early childhood classroom environments, *The Reading Teacher*, 44 (6).

NCC (1991) *Report on Monitoring the Implementation of the National Curriculum Core Subjects: 1989–90*. York: National Curriculum Council.

Opie, I. and Opie, P. (1959) *The Lore and Language of School Children*. Oxford: Oxford University Press.

Pearson, H. (1990) Stories and Learning to Read, *Reading*, 24 (2).

Phillips, M. (1990) Educashun still isn't working, *The Guardian*, 28 September.

Robinson, A. (1989) But we still believe in Father Christmas. In N. Hall (ed.) *Writing with Reason: The Emergence of Authorship in Young Children*. London: Hodder and Stoughton.

SCDC (1989) *Becoming a Writer*. Walton-on-Thames: Thomas Nelson.

Smith, F. (1971) *Understanding Reading*. New York: Holt, Rinehart, and Winston.

Smith, F. (1978) *Reading*. Cambridge: Cambridge University Press.

Southgate, V. (1968) Formulae for beginning reading tuition, *Educational Research*, 10 (1).

Southgate, V., Arnold, H. and Johnson, S. (1981) *Extending Beginning Reading*. London: Heinemann Educational.

Strickland, D. S. and Morrow, L. M. (1989) Interactive experiences with storybook reading, *The Reading Teacher*, 42 (5).

Teale, W. H. (1984) Reading to young children: its significance for literacy development. In H. Goelman, A. A. Oberg and F. Smith (eds) *Awakening to Literacy*. London: Heinemann Educational.

Teale, W. H. (1988) Reading their way to reading, *Reading Today*, 5 (6).

Tizard, B. and Hughes, M. (1984) *Young Children Learning: Talking and Thinking at Home and at School*. London: Fontana Paperbacks.

Torrey, J. W. (1969) Learning to read without a teacher: a case study, *Elementary English*, 46.

Trelease, J. (1984) *The Read Aloud Handbook*. Harmondsworth: Penguin.

Turner, M. (1990) *Sponsored Reading Failure*. Warlingham: IPSET Education Unit.

Wade, B. (1990) Reading from home to school. In B. Wade (ed.) *Reading for Real*. Milton Keynes: Open University Press.

Waterland, L. (1988) *Read With Me: An Apprenticeship Approach to Reading*. Stroud: Thimble Press.

Wells, G. (1985) Language and learning: an interactional perspective. In G. Wells and J. Nicholls (eds) *Language and Learning: An Interactional Perspective*. Lewes: Falmer Press.

Wells, G. (1986) *The Meaning Makers: Children Learning Language and Using Language to Learn*. London: Hodder and Stoughton.

Wheldall, K. and Entwistle, J. (1988) Back in the USSR: the effect of teacher modelling of silent reading on pupil's reading behaviour in the primary school classroom, *Educational Psychology*, 8.

White, D. N. (1984) *Books before Five*. Portsmouth, New Hampshire: Heinemann Educational.

Whitehead, M. (1987) Reading – caught or taught?, *English in Education*, 21 (2).

Whitehead, M. (1988) Narrative, stories and the world of literature. In G. M. Blenkin and A. V. Kelly (eds) *Early Childhood Education: A Developmental Curriculum*. London: Paul Chapman.

Wilkinson, A., Barnsley, G., IIanna, P. and Swan, M. (1980) *Assessing Language Development*. Oxford: Oxford University Press.

Wray, D. and Medwell, J. (1991) *Literacy and Language in the Primary Years*. London: Routledge.

Index